This is the heartrending, true story of a grandmother's love for her rebellious, reckless, ne'er-do-well grandson of nineteen and her dedicated efforts to help him establish himself as a law-abiding citizen in the world. To accomplish this, she, at the age of eighty, invites him to come live with her after he has left his own home where he cannot get along with his parents. Unbelievable as some incidents may seem to be, nothing has been concocted. The account is true in all its details, even to the twice fortuitous ringing of the telephone bell in critical moments.

Here are elements that make a story really worth reading: suspense, humor, hope, despair, aspiration. Here are the emotional revelations of a boy's struggle to free himself from the dangerous habit of dependence on drugs. And here are the grandmother's patient, stubborn, and sometimes dangerous risks to help him in that pitiful struggle. But most of all, here is the story of a spiritual journey from darkness to light, from doubt to belief, and a recognition of the Power that has directed everything from the very beginning—the Power that lies beyond love, the Power of Faith.

In CALL IF YOU NEED ME, Mary Randall provides no phony finale, no happy ending. Rather, she quietly says something tremendously important about families, about close relationships, about the agonies of temptation, and about the real meaning of caring. And, unconsciously, she tells the reader a great deal about

Call if you need me

MARY RANDALL

FLEMING H. REVELL COMPANY
Old Tappan, New Jersey

Scripture references in this volume are from the King James Version of the Bible.

Library of Congress Cataloging in Publication Data

Randall, Mary.
    Call if you need me.

    I. Title.
PZ3.C7253Cal [PS3505.03769]   813'.5'2   76–41683
ISBN 0–8007–0845–8

Childhood scenes . . . such memories are the key not to the past, but to the future . . . when we let God use them [they] become the mysterious and perfect preparation for the work He will give us to do.

. . . certain moments from long ago stood out in focus against the blur of years. Oddly sharp and near they were, as though they were not yet finished, as though they had something more to say. . . .

CORRIE TEN BOOM
The Hiding Place

Prologue

This is the true story of a grandmother's love for her rebellious, reckless, ne'er-do-well grandson of nineteen and her dedicated efforts to help him establish himself as a law-abiding citizen in the world. To accomplish this, she, at the age of eighty, invites him to come live with her after he has left his own home, where he cannot get along with his parents. Unbelievable as some incidents may seem to be, nothing has been concocted. Everything that happened is based on diaries she kept and letters she sent to an interested social worker who later returned them to her. It is, indeed, true in all its details, even to the twice fortuitous ringing of the telephone bell in critical moments.

Here are suspense, humor, hope, despair, and aspiration. Here are the revelations of a boy's struggle to free himself from the dangerous habit of dependence on drugs. And here are the grandmother's patient, stubborn, and sometimes dangerous risks to help him in that struggle. But most of all, here is the story of a spiritual journey from darkness to light, from doubt to belief, and a recognition of the Power that has directed everything from the very beginning—the Power that lies beyond love, the Power of Faith.

THE PUBLISHERS

1

I must work the works of him that sent me. . . .

John 9:4

I didn't know at all what to do that day. Even though I was eighty years old and had learned a good deal in my long life, I still didn't know what to do. So I just kept on driving. Beside me in my old Chevy, my nineteen-year-old grandson sat as silent as I, his expression one of grim defiance. But the situation was serious. Something ought to be done. I was sure of that much though nothing more.

In such an impasse it had become a habit with me to keep still and wait. Keep perfectly still—and wait. Usually, then, an idea would occur to me on which I could act. This is what happened now. Only it was all backward. For ahead of the idea came words, without either my volition or intention. I heard myself saying them though I had not yet even thought them. And they were stupid. Right away I was aware of that. Because where could they lead? Exactly nowhere. Yes. Stupid. But I had had to say them. I hadn't been able to help myself. It was as if someone else were in my skin speaking for me.

"Gregory darling, if you don't want to live at home with your mom and dad any more, would you like to come live with me? Or do you think that I would hassle you too?"

His answer came promptly. "No! You wouldn't. You never have. I'd like that. But I don't know. I'll have to think about it and tell you tomorrow. Stop here, Gram. I'll get off here by the monument. My room's not far. And thanks for the lift."

He gave me his slow, sweet smile, unfolded his legs, slipped out, and was gone. His tall, slim figure, moving with his customary arrogant grace, was lost to my sight in a moment, as he had wanted it to be. I wasn't to know just exactly where he would be in this neighboring town he had chosen to live in from now on. Despite the empathy that had existed between us ever since he was twelve, that had always made communication between us possible, and that assured him of the strength of my love for him, I was not wholly trusted.

I drove on, still astonished at myself. And at him too, for surely he should have given me an abrupt turndown. It had been a preposterous thought. But he had not so treated it. Was he just being his usual polite self to me? This was always endearing.

My thoughts now centered on Gregory. He was a lawless, reckless rebel and had been a heartbreaking problem to us all in his family for years. Yet I clung—now as always—to the invincible belief that in time he would change his ways and become what I knew he could be. Love would bring this to pass. So many things had been tried and had failed! But love would work the miracle. If tomorrow he should tell me that he would come to me, would that be the beginning of the miracle? I had no idea any more than I had any idea what he would say. My mind was a blank. Even so, I made myself now consider the feasibility of his joining me, however impossible this might seem. I was a widow living alone in a one-bedroom apartment. The rooms were large and a corner situation gave good crosscurrents of air. In my good-sized bedroom were twin beds, while in the spacious living room there was a sofa bed that opened out into a full double. A good-sized closet in the dining area would hold all Gregory's possessions. We would not be crowded anywhere, I thought. I could still have privacy. Yes, everything would be all right. We could be comfortable. I could manage—if he came.

If.

My mind went back to what had precipitated this situation. Not a half hour ago I had entered my daughter's kitchen to ask her if she wanted me to get anything for her when I went shopping in Edgewood, the next town, where I was heading. I found her at her sink, furiously scrubbing a large dirt-encrusted fry pan and I knew at once by the violence of her motions that the source of her anger was Gregory again. She exploded into speech.

"Gregory *just* came in! Not ten minutes ago! He's been away this whole weekend and I had no idea *where!* He didn't telephone me! He never does! And Friday night—I had told him! He knew!—I had prepared his favorite dinner for him and I'd said he could ask Ellen if he wanted to. I was trying to let him know I was glad he'd landed this church job even if it isn't much. But he never showed up. Not Friday night or all day Saturday or Sunday. Not until just now. He doesn't *care* how he upsets me! I try to do something to please him and he throws it back in my face. He thinks his life is his own to do as he pleases and I'm to let him alone. But, Mother! How can I? When he's so irresponsible? When most of the time he acts about ten years old?" She paused for breath.

"He did say he'd gone to work on Friday," she went on, after a moment. "When he didn't turn up for dinner that night I was sure he'd chucked the job and didn't come home because he didn't want to tell me. I knew he wasn't keen to take it. But he's been without anything so long now! Months! All summer! He hasn't even had money for cigarettes. He cadges off his friends or helps himself here from mine. So I was glad when he told me he'd worked both Thursday and Friday—and today too." She lifted up the fry pan, rinsed it, laid it on the drainboard, and let the water run out of the sink.

"He'd better stay with it," she continued. "Neither the minister nor Moe really wanted to take him on. They know his record. But I guess they were sorry for Tom and me, or else thought it was their Christian duty. Anyway, Moe telephoned late Wednesday evening to tell Greg he was to be a kind of assistant custodian to him—Moe—on a part-time basis." She faced me. "Well! Do you think Gregory showed he was pleased? Do you think he even said thank you? I'll tell you what he said! I was standing right next to him by the phone and he drawled out in that infuriating way of his, 'Do I have to work Saturdays? If I do, I'm not interested.' I wanted to hit him! *Honestly!*" She whipped a towel from a rod on the kitchen door and dried her hands. "*Honestly!*" she repeated. "You'd think *he* was doing the favor! And let me tell you one more thing. I had to call him six times—*six times*— the next morning before I could get him awake to go his first day. And he argued and raved at me every single minute till I finally pushed him out the door." She blew out a totally exasperated breath and stopped at last.

I said nothing. It was too familiar, for this was what went on between them all the time. They simply could not get along. She tried to direct and control and he would take neither. So they lived in a vortex of frustration and animosity. Flaring tempers, threats, defiance, suspicion and mistrust were the order of the day. I ached for both of them. While I was searching for some words of comfort and kindness, she spoke again. But her voice was no longer angry. It sounded simply very tired.

"Mother, if he loses this job—I can't stand it. He's lost—or given up—so many, and I tell you I can't stand it." She pushed her hair away from her face and let out a sigh. "He's upstairs. Taking a shower. That's all he came home for. That—and clean clothes. I still don't know where he was this past weekend or where he's going now or his plans for tonight about eating here. I don't know anything. He won't tell me. He won't talk."

"I'll talk." Gregory had appeared in the doorway. He stood there, bearded and burnished, his wavy bronze hair, glistening with drops of water, neatly brushed and tied back on his neck, his big brown eyes, so clear, so *honest*. My heart twisted at the potential of splendor that he presented, a potential unguessed by him but dreamed of, hoped for, and believed in by me.

He said, addressing me, not his mother, "I've been in Edgewood. Making arrangements for living there. I'm not going to stay under this roof anymore. I've taken a room in a commune. With about nine or ten others, whites and blacks. We all chip in on food, and the woman who owns the house will cook for us. It'll cost me thirty-five dollars a week."

I heard Fern gasp. Gregory's part-time job was to bring him only forty dollars. He had no money saved and no car for transportation. His mother—feeling, as always, responsible for his welfare, so she must at least *try* to reason with him—said, "Greg! Are you crazy? How can you pay for any food? Why don't you—"

He cut in, still without looking at her, and asked me with his usual courtesy if I would mind taking him partway to Edgewood. He'd thought he had heard me say I was going shopping there.

I had nodded, my heart grieving for Fern, so insultingly ignored, so helpless before his obduracy, so clearly hated—and now struck to a silence that left her looking broken as I had never seen her. I said, nodding at her, "I'll be back," and Gregory and I had departed.

I found out no more than she had. But even so, I knew more. For when we had retired our cook a number of years ago, before my husband died, she had lived until her death in the area where Gregory was going. It was known as the ghetto and I remembered it clearly. The dangling light bulb, the bare, splintered floor, the scuttling cockroaches, the dripping cold-water faucet in the kitchen, the toilet with a door that never shut tight, so there was always the smell of urine in the air. Gregory had been reared in comfort and cleanliness. He had come home for a shower after only a weekend there. How long could he stand such surroundings?

I remembered, too, the racial animosities that smoldered there and that, breaking into the open, had put Edgewood on the front pages more than once. I knew of the fires and holdups and rapings and killings that were going on there now and that kept the town on edge and fearful all the time. And I knew, too, that Gregory, though completely democratic, was quick-tempered, and that he carried a large, wicked-looking hunting knife tucked down in his belt. It had been on him today. It was because of all these thoughts that I had asked him to come live with me.

His reply, so swift, so surprising, had given me a chance for only the briefest glimpse of the possible difficulties and ramifications that might result should he accept. But I had made the offer and there was no retreat, since I could not deny my love for this grandson of mine who was living so chaotically, whose past held so little that was commendable and whose future promised not much better, yet in whom I had a curious faith. These were the constants of my life. So all I could do was wait for his decision.

What would it be? I simply could not guess.

The next morning, over my cup of coffee, Fern's words came back to me. I had returned to her after my shopping as I had said I would and found her even more tense and anguished than earlier, though her fire had died.

"He'll lose this job, too. I know it. He'll never wake up in the morning. Someone—Tom or I—always has to call him, and then it's like pulling teeth to get him down for breakfast. I've told you! Oh, it's all so idiotic! The whole thing! Practically every cent going to pay for that room! He'll have nothing for food! He could *save* his money here! And I wouldn't ask him to pay board. I never have. And there's another thing. From here he could walk to the church in five minutes. But Edgewood is over two miles away—and with no car—" She broke off. "This has gone on too long," she had finished in a low, slow voice. "I can't take it anymore, Mother. Neither can Tom. We're tired. Tired of giving and forgiving. Tired of his fighting with us over everything. Tired of his foolish plans or sudden notions that never pan out. Tired of his drinking and his shouting and the police coming around all the time. Why do they come? They're suspicious of him. They think he's back of a lot of things that go on in this town. Who knows what he does when he doesn't come home till two or three in the morning? We don't! And we don't want to know. But if he's fired now"—she drew a breath—"we're through, Mother. We've decided that. We're really *through*. We've done everything possible for him, and nothing has been any good. So we're through."

And there had been no doubting the finality of her words. Remembering them now, I put down my cup and rose. My car was parked in front of my apartment door. I got into it, started the motor, and headed for the main road between our village and Edgewood. My watch said eight-forty. It would take about five minutes—maybe less —to reach the monument. Plenty of time to run him to the church. If he was up. If he was even awake! Or if he hadn't already hitchhiked. Perhaps I shouldn't be doing this. But he had said he would tell me today and I had to know. Oh, it was all too dangerous! Too unbearable!

I saw his striding figure a block away before he saw me. Flinging up an arm when he recognized my car, he called out, "Hi, Gram! I'm glad you came. How did you happen to?" Without waiting for an answer, he said as he got in beside me, "I've decided. I'll come live with you."

Just like that. A momentous decision, a bombshell, really, tossed to me most casually. And because I had learned how to meet him, I gave a little laugh and accepted it in the same way.

"Good. Tonight, you mean?"

"Yes. Will you get my clothes for me? I only have what's on me."

"As soon as I leave you at the church now."

He gave me a small crooked smile. "I'd be late today if you hadn't come."

"That's what I figured."

"Gram, I haven't had any breakfast except some wine. And only potato chips for dinner last night."

"Well, I brought along a couple of sandwiches for your coffee break. And we'll pick up a carton of chocolate milk on the way if you like."

"Oh, good! Thanks. Will you explain to Mom?"

"Yes. When I go for your clothes. What time shall I look for you?"

A foolish question. Time meant nothing to him. He said he didn't know but I wasn't to wait dinner for him.

So we left it. I dropped him at the church and then went to see my daughter and break the news to her.

Fern was, of course, appalled.

"Mother! You can't *do* this! You just can't! You didn't tell me yesterday that you'd asked him! Why in the world did you! It's crazy! You have no idea what it'll be like! His hours are awful. You never know when he'll come in—or if he even will! You'll wait up and wait up and get no sleep—"

"I don't need much. Five hours is enough."

"Mother! Please *listen!* It's an insane idea! You're eighty! And lame! You have that arthritic hip that bothers you. Forget it, will you? Tom won't like it at all. He's fond of you. And have you forgotten that Gregory drinks? When he does—he's impossible. You've never seen him. But he'll yell at you and say awful things, even though he loves you as much as he loves anybody. Mother, please! Tell him you've changed your mind."

I said, "Fern, I must try. That's all. I must try."

But she pushed on. "And he takes downers. To get to sleep. Then, in the morning—oh, I've said all this! But there's another thing. You'll have Ellen on your neck. She'll drive you wild, the way she did us."

"Nobody is going to drive me wild," I answered. "Now please go pack his clothes."

I had met Gregory's girl friend several times. She was tall, red-haired—she had beautiful long, thick red hair—and she was chic. I had found her to be noncommittal, indeed quite reserved, so I had come to no conclusions about her. I had formed no judgments.

Fern was still trying to think of more arguments. I wanted them to end. I said, "Fern, this is an experiment. I realize that. But my way with Gregory will be different from yours. When I was living with you those few years after Dad died, he and I got along beautifully. Remember? What I mean is—I'm not his mother, as you are, so I don't have to *shape* him. I only have to *accept* him." I paused. Had I hit on some truth? I went on gently. "The thing is that Gregory has left you. He's *left* you, my dear. He's chosen me. And I love him."

Fern had the last word. "Well, you know what the psychiatrist and the minister said about that: 'Love is not enough.'"

But I had never agreed. I felt it could be. It must be! It *would* be —because I would make it be.

I had great confidence in myself.

Gregory had said, "Don't wait dinner for me," so I hadn't. I had just finished my own and must now pass the time until he appeared. I still did not wholly believe he would come. He had told me he would, yes—but he could change his mind for some reason. Or, indeed, for no reason. You could never count on him. I had been foolish to believe him.

I sank into my blue wing chair and picked up my crewel work to pass the time. It had been a busy day. I had put away Gregory's clothes after I had brought them from Fern's house, had hung fresh towels in the bathroom, had made up the sofa bed with clean sheets, and then had gone out to shop for food. All Gregory's favorite items were now awaiting his pleasure in my fridge or on my kitchen shelves. Milk, peanut butter, bacon, eggs, potato crinkles, cereals, and thin sandwich steaks for the large round rolls he liked.

I glanced at the clock. Only five past eight. After a long while it was eight-thirty. When would he come? Or wouldn't he? Just then the phone rang. It was Fern. Had Gregory arrived yet? No. "Mother, I *worry.*" I told her to stop her worrying and not to call me again. I would call her. And she must absolutely leave us *alone.* She said, "He'll bring Ellen with him. What will you do if he does?" I replied that I would let her know after that happened. Then I hung up.

But her words came back to me through the silence as they so often did. These were the words she had spoken before I had left her this afternoon. "It won't work," she had said. "I know it won't. If it doesn't, Tom and I will understand and you mustn't feel too badly. Gregory has his room here, you know. And he has a key to our house." She finished slowly, her voice holding a sadness that hurt me to hear, "We don't *want* to throw him out, Mother. He's our *son.*"

I glanced at the clock now. Not yet nine. Well, nine was early, of course. I picked up my crewel work once more—not thinking, not hoping, not expecting—just waiting, living in a vacuum. Nine-thirty. Nine-forty-five—

At a little after ten my musical doorbell sounded. I opened my door and there stood Gregory. He was alone.

"Hi, Gram," he said. He was as casual as before. So was I, though relief and joy surged up in me tumultuously. I put my arms around him, feeling his thinness, and kissed him warmly.

"Darling, I'm *so* glad to see you! Are you hungry?"

"Well—"

"Come out into the kitchen and see if there's anything you want."

He ate a toasted meat sandwich and drank nearly a quart of milk. Afterward I showed him where I had put his clothes and he pulled open the sofa bed. He said very little and I could see he was terribly tired. I didn't in the least like his looks.

"I brought over your small radio," I told him. "You can plug it in here. It just fits on the table by your bed."

"Thanks. I'd like to turn on your TV too, if you don't mind. I don't get to sleep much before two o'clock."

"Maybe you will tonight. But turn it on if you want. Just keep it low. Shall I waken you in the morning?"

"Perhaps you'd better."

I kissed him again and went to my room and closed my door. Through it, I could not hear the TV at all.

My experiment with Gregory had begun. How challenging it would be I had no idea. But anyway, he was here. And Ellen had not been mentioned.

In the silence of my room I found myself going over the past two days. They had been strange in more ways than one. Take first my stopping at Fern's instead of telephoning her as I had first thought I would do. If I hadn't gone, I wouldn't have encountered Gregory in her kitchen, and I wouldn't have given him a ride in my car, and there would have been no invitation to him to come live with me. Had it been chance?

Take also that later moment when, out of the blue, out of my ignorance of what to do, I had spoken, surprising myself with my words. *My* words? When I hadn't even *thought* them?

I had been *led* to Fern's. I had been *made* to speak. And Gregory had been *moved* to accept my invitation. What was going on? Who had taken over our lives? God? Yes. God.

I thought about Him as a memory came to me.

I was standing alone before my minister, the only one of my Sunday-school class to join the church that day, and suddenly I was filled with a lofty joy. I did not understand it. I only knew that, without warning, I had become aware of God's goodness to me. I had wise and loving parents because He had given them to me. He had given me my friends too. And all the small successes and triumphs I had known in the various activities I had entered, had been mine because He had created me. "My cup runneth over," I had thought, and in that moment's delirium of happiness, I came to a swift decision. I owed a great debt to God, therefore all my prayers would, in the future, contain only words of thanks. Just thanks. Nothing else. And never, never would I *ask* for anything—for He had already given me more than my share, so it would not be fair. It was a curious, adolescent, and entirely emotional resolution that I made in the blink of an eye that Sunday morning, but it was sincerely entered into and, indeed, became my credo. God, hitherto a dim Deity, only perfunctorily addressed as I knelt by my bed at night and requiring my weekly presence at Sunday school, was, though still remote, very real to me in that experience.

So now as I lay in the darkness of my bedroom, remembering this from long ago, I sent my heartfelt thanks heavenward because Gregory had come to live with me that day.

2

And God is able to make all grace abound toward you. . . .

2 Corinthians 9:8

The next morning I woke Gregory with a kiss. He rolled over and did not open his eyes. I knew he had watched TV until two o'clock. I knew five hours of sleep was not enough for him. I knew he was run down from haphazard meals, too much drinking, and possibly drugs. Indeed Fern had spoken of "downers," but the word meant little to me. What I did know, though, was that he could hardly pull himself together now to go to do the half-day's work that lay ahead of him. I knew too—and this was the most important of all—that he had come to me in the belief that I would not "hassle" him.

What did that word mean, exactly? It meant I must not nag, correct, advise, question, criticize, or oppose him on any matter. I must let him feel absolutely free to do as he pleased. At the same time I must somehow get him up now, get him to eat a decent breakfast, get him to church on time. Fern had said it would be a battle. And the battle had begun. Yet it must not be a battle. How would I work this out?

I leaned over and kissed him again, asked what kind of warm cereal he would like, told him the hour it was, and went to the kitchen. I myself am always prompt for any appointment I might have, so it was not easy for me to see the minutes slipping away and Gregory making no move to bestir himself. Had he gone to sleep again? I must not call to find out, for that would be hassling. So I just began talking. I rattled on about everything except the time. Presently I took his cereal bowl to his bedside, along with milk and sugar for it, a roll, and a small glass of orange juice. "I'm spoiling you," I said, smiling down at him. "Do you want me to feed you too?"

I thought of my Ted at that point. Unbidden, he sprang to my mind. Ted, my firstborn, who had been a mongoloid. It was Ted who had taught me the patience I had needed to have with him. How many times had I folded his small resistant fingers about the curved handle of his silver baby spoon, guided his little fist to pick up a scoop of food from his thick-rimmed bowl, guided the spoon to his mouth. Over and over for every bite, for every meal, for every day, for every week for more than a year—until the repeated motion made a groove or pattern in his mind and he was finally able to feed himself. (This was just before Fern was born, when Ted was a little over two and still not walking or talking.) What weary elation I had felt when the brain specialist whom we had finally consulted had said to me, "That was the only right and possible way to teach him. How did you know?" I hadn't known. It had been instinct with me. I had just *felt* what to do.

So now I felt what to do with Gregory. It seemed silly, but nothing else occurred to me. So I pretended I would feed him. Of course he wouldn't allow it—"What do you think you're *doing,* Gram?"—and presently he had finished eating and had dragged himself up to dress. We made it to the church without a minute to spare, and with Moe watching our approach while his eyes kept turning to the clock high above his head. He was fussy about punctuality. Beside me, Gregory was still only half awake.

"Good morning, Moe," I said. And then—"Greg darling, here's your snack for the coffee break. I'll come back for you at one. O.K?"

He nodded. But Moe, listening, did not approve. He had been in our church for many years and knew me well enough to speak his mind. Why was I coddling this boy that way? It wasn't right! Here I was driving him to his job! Wasn't he old enough at nineteen to get himself there? And to come for him too! Be good for him to walk those two or three blocks to my apartment when he finished his work. I only smiled at his tirade and shook my head, for I knew better than he the shape Gregory was in. Besides, he could easily be sidetracked by some one he knew along the way, and I didn't want that at all. It was my hope that with a good breakfast, the midmorning snack, and a nourishing lunch when he came back to me, he would soon feel much better. Yes, a few days or weeks of that— Confidently I left my thought unfinished.

I went home and spent the morning tidying up my apartment, washing out some sox and underthings for Gregory, telephoning a friend or two, and preparing the noon meal I had planned. A few minutes before one, I drove down to the church, parked in the rear near the door from which Gregory would emerge, and blew my horn. It was Moe who came out to me.

Gregory had gone, he told me. He had finished the work Moe had given him to do, so he had left a bit early. Maybe five minutes ago.

I thanked him and started back, wondering why I hadn't passed him somewhere. Well, perhaps he had cut through and was walking along the railroad tracks. No doubt he had forgotten I was to go for him and he would be waiting impatiently at my locked door when I reached it. I must give him a key, I thought then.

But he was not waiting at the door. Had he gone by way of the village for cigarettes? Probably. I don't smoke, so I had none to offer him when he asked last night. Yes, that was it. Well—he would be back soon then. I let myself in and waited awhile for him. Still he did not appear. But surely he must be hungry! Surely for that reason he would turn up in a few more minutes! But he didn't. I let ten go by, then another ten—and at last reluctantly I gave up, ate my own lunch and put his away. I was provoked a little but not disturbed or surprised. I had known he couldn't be counted on. Not for anything at any time. I knew that perfectly well! I knew exactly what he was like. Why should I think he had changed overnight? I was expecting too much too soon.

The afternoon was long. And the evening, after my solitary supper, was longer. I decided to telephone Fern as I had said I would. But I dodged some of her inquiries. Yes, Gregory had gone to work on time. And—yes—there'd been no fuss at breakfast. We were getting along all right. No blowups. No swearing. Nothing. He was out now but I expected him in soon. Any minute. I did not say a word about the luncheon fiasco. She was not to know all that happened—or didn't happen—here. She would just worry.

I went back to my waiting after I had hung up. But questions kept revolving in my mind. Gregory! Where are you? Why didn't you come home at noon? Why aren't you here now? What are you doing? Why don't you at least telephone me? Let me know a little *something*— Somehow this time of waiting was worse than last night had been.

And reading no more possible now than then.

For a second time in my life I had a problem boy in my care. And for the second time since he had been with me, my thoughts turned back to the first one—my Ted.

He had been nearly five before we came to know the full truth about him. He *looked* so perfectly normal! Yet he was developing much too slowly and no local doctor could give us an explanation. When finally the New York specialist broke it to us I could not believe it. My blond, blue-eyed, beautiful boy, so gentle, so lovable, not to grow up to full manhood? It was simply not true.

But it was true. Inevitably I came to know this for there was daily proof. Ted never matured mentally past his seventh year though he lived into his forties. He dwelt in a sheltered world all that time, protected to a large extent by his own unawareness. Yet he was extraordinarily, almost uncannily, sensitive. It was as if—sometimes —he could read our minds and moods, so I had always to be most careful lest my tone betray my impatience and he, troubled, think that my love, his only bulwark against a puzzling world, had been withdrawn. Oh, indeed, yes! I had, in pain and heartbreak and through a dark and dreadful period that seemed unending, learned patience with Ted. Was that why he had been sent me? So that, because of what he had taught me, I should now be ready for Gregory?

I did not know. But I remembered clearly that in my shock and grief I had not once cried out my anguish or asked for strength to bear it. When our minister called to offer me comfort, he had said, "You will need help. Shall we pray?" And though I bent my head in acquiescence, I did not hear the words he spoke or join him in thought, for I was remembering a pledge I had made long years ago. *Give thanks but never, never ask for anything.* It had been a pledge steadfastly kept —and easily so. Four years of happiness at college, a chosen career begun with unusual success, and a good marriage. Yes, it had been easy. Indeed, thankfulness had become a well-entrenched habit—until Ted came. Then, because of him, I could not give thanks. Nor could I ask for help. Indeed, what could God do? It was He who had sent this child to me, and I had accepted him with love and pity in my heart but no rebellion. Still, I could not pray. Not at that moment with the minister or, in fact, later—for God, though the source of many gifts to me, was still a distant figure. So I kept silent until—finally—

I found a reason for thankfulness.

I came to see, in time, that my straight-backed, sturdy boy was not one from whom people shrank. What he evoked, with his good looks, his dimpled smile, his sweet and friendly ways, was interest, tenderness, and a warm affection. He made friends. He hurt no one. He could, then, live in the world with us. He could stay within the family. He need not be hidden or put away—as had been advised.

This realization brought with it a challenge. But I had met challenges before—in my school years, in the profession I had entered, in my married life, and, despite the difficulties they presented, I had, in meeting them, managed usually to achieve a measure of success. Better yet, I had found my own strength. So now I thought that though it might be a misfortune to have a mongoloid son, it need not be a catastrophe. Something could be done—and I would do it. I would build on Ted's assets. I would bring him to the highest level he could reach. I would make a tragedy less tragic.

Having so decided—what was to be done? First, root out any bitterness or anger I might have in my heart. But there was none and never had been. I had known only a numbing despair, which was now being dissipated by my newly discovered goal. To reach that, I must study, read, *learn,* and find the best way to train and teach my handicapped son. I must help him find his own niche in life. I would never give up. And these efforts, both of mind and spirit, were put forth by me with a desperate, determined intensity which occupied me so exclusively that I completely forgot how to laugh. For nearly two years I forgot there was such a thing as laughter in the world.

And then one day I saw, with new and startled eyes, my darling dancing daughter with her red-gold hair, quick grace, and bright unquenchable joyousness—and I realized with a stab of compunction that I was *her* mother too, and that she had a right to receive from me more than a grim fortitude (my unconscious demeanor) and compulsory attention to her physical needs. She was living as much as Ted. I recalled how my first attempt to respond smilingly to her gaiety had made me clap my hands to my cheeks when I felt the unconscious pull and stretch of long-unused muscles. It was a strange and frightening feeling. But it brought me alive once more.

And if God's name had passed my lips during that black interval, it was (I thought) as a kind of smothered groan to which I would not, because I could not, give words. It was an emotional release, nothing more. Certainly it had not been complaint and neither was it an appeal. For hadn't it been up to me? I had believed so.

I stirred in my chair. All that was in what now seemed another era. It was a life remembered as if lived by someone other than me. And though it had been no triumph, it was no disaster either. What that long travail had given me was the discovery, the *certainty,* that I could cope with whatever came to me. So now I would cope with Gregory. Ted was gone. But I was still here. And the present was pressing heavily on me.

I was back where I had started—thinking of Gregory. Another firstborn. Another problem. Yet how different! Ted's lack had been easily visible when one watched closely. There was no lack visible in Gregory. He seemed, rather, to have too much of everything. Too much vitality, curiosity, fearlessness, lust for living. Only it was all so random! So undirected and explosive! So pointless and, in the end, so harmful to himself. Fern and Tom had tried everything to bring his behavior into acceptable lines, to fit him into society. They had sought and followed the best advice available from doctors, educators, psychiatrists, and ministers. They had tried a summer camp under the auspices of the church we attended—and had met with disappointment. They had tried schools which had seemed to offer help—and had received none. "Nobody is going to change me!" Gregory had declared stormily once. And nobody did. Though successful with their second son, Bruce, they had failed with Gregory.

And now, as things had worked out, it was my turn to try. Could I succeed where they'd failed? Could I, through the love I felt for my grandson, bring *him* to *his* highest level?

Love is not enough. Was that true? If it was, what more was needed? I did not know. So many things I didn't know! What was the good of getting old if you were no wiser?

I let out an impatient sigh and looked at my watch. Midnight had passed while I had been dreaming. Well, Gregory wasn't going to appear tonight, I felt sure. This was not unusual, Fern had told me. But it was hard to accept. Oh, Gregory darling, why aren't you here? Why did you say you would like to live with me and then leave me right away? Why, Gregory? *Why?*

I didn't know the answer to that either.

In the morning I drove toward the monument, looking for Gregory as I had yesterday. I might find him today again too. It was possible. It was worth a chance.

Sure enough, there he was, plodding along the sidewalk without any of his usual spring and as if he could hardly move himself along. He seemed glad to see me when I stopped to pick him up, and as he got into my car he said redundantly, "I didn't come back to you last night."

I answered amusedly, "So I noticed."

"I haven't had any breakfast."

"Not even wine?"

"I didn't feel like it this morning."

"Well, I think there's time to stop at my apartment for a quick bite."

Silence. Then— "I was at Artie's."

"Artie's?"

"Yes. He's in the house his mother owns, where I had the room. Ellen was there too."

Ellen. We had come to Ellen. I waited.

"Her car's not fixed yet. She has to stay at Artie's sometimes to check on it."

"I see," I said, as if I did.

There was another silence. Perhaps because I made no comment and asked no questions, he became talkative.

"Her car got smashed up in New York one night. We were mixed up in a kind of riot. I'll tell you sometime. I got it back to Edgewood okay and now a friend of Artie's is going to put it in shape cheaper than the Volkswagen garage would do it. But it's going to take time. That's why she has to be there. To check up on it because he's so slow and we're in a hurry to get it fixed. And when she's there I don't like her to be alone at night without me, because she's white."

"No, of course not. And I'm glad you feel protective about her. Only—why can't she go home?"

"Gram! I just told you! She has no car! And she lives *miles* from here! About thirty. Anyway, she hates her parents. She doesn't want to go home. Artie took her there in his car when I came to you night before last."

"I see," I said again.

"So until her car gets fixed we're renting a little U-Haul truck, and then she can go back and forth. Because she has to get clean clothes and take a shower and wash her hair now and then."

I could not answer, for I was struck dumb with astonishment. How in the world were they going to pay for the rental of a U-Haul truck out of Gregory's paltry forty dollars a week? I was appalled at his lack of common sense, his complete inability to put first things first. He simply had no balance when it came to money. Again—as in so many other instances—he had leaped without looking. But *don't comment,* I warned myself. *Don't ask questions. Don't give any advice.*

He continued. He was giving me information as long as I kept silent. Sparingly, to be sure, but he was giving it. "That's why I didn't get back to you last night. We were making arrangements about the U-Haul and then it was too late. Artie's helping us."

So that was how. I said, "Artie sounds like a good friend."

"He is, Gram. He's a nice guy. He lends us money when we need it. He always has money. He takes us in to New York in his car sometimes too, when we want to go. He's a real nice guy."

"What does he do to make his money?"

"Nothing. He's a war veteran. He's had major surgery done on him and he was in a hospital for a long time when he got back from Vietnam. So now he gets a check from the government every month. He can't breathe very well to talk. It makes his voice sound funny."

We reached my apartment. Hurriedly I gave him some cold cereal and a drink of Carnation milk and off we went to the church. I was thinking of Ellen all the way. If she was going to stay in Edgewood at Artie's house while her car was being fixed and if Gregory wasn't willing to leave her there at night alone, how was he going to go on living with me? What good was my offer of a home to him? What earthly good? *You'll have Ellen on your neck,* Fern had warned me.

At the church I faced my grandson.

"Gregory, if you don't want to leave Ellen alone, I'd rather you brought her to my apartment than stay down at Artie's when she has to be there."

He got out of the car without answering. I wasn't sure he had heard me. I wasn't sure I had said what I had. Or indeed what I meant by it. So I was glad he hadn't answered. It gave me a breathing spell in which to think.

3

Be ye kind one to another, tenderhearted, forgiving one another.

Ephesians 4:32

Gregory was with me that night—Thursday—for the U-Haul had taken Ellen to her distant home and she would not be returning until Saturday. Gregory told me this while he was eating something in my kitchen late that night. I had joined him there and had been given a little more information.

Ellen hated her parents, he said again. Especially her father. She was having to pay him so much every month because he had financed the purchase of her car, and if she was late with her payment he would probably take it away from her. He didn't know a thing about this accident or he would surely take it. Then he would sell it. If that happened, he and Ellen would have no way to get around. His car was smashed long ago.

"We've got to have a car, Gram. We've just *got* to! She's *got* to have hers fixed." He was silent a moment. "Ellen has her unemployment check. She gets one every two weeks but I'm not entitled to any. I've never worked at any place long enough. Well, with her check she has to pay her father—and Artie's friend who's doing her car—and something for her room—and food—" He broke off. "Well! It isn't *all* up to her! I have to help her! I use the car as much as she does, so I feel it's half mine and that I have to pay my share!" He broke off again. Then— "Gram! I've simply got to make more money than I get at the church! I've got to work in the afternoons too." There was a repressed desperation in his voice. I could see he felt driven and as if he were only half a man. Yet he was not in any shape to do a full day's work. Not yet. I offered what help I could think of.

"Maybe you can pick up some odd jobs here and there until you can line up something regular for your afternoons. Listen, Gregory. I'm remembering something. Right now I have a friend who wants some painting done around one window at her apartment. If you're free tomorrow afternoon—if Ellen won't be back till Saturday—do you want to do that bit of work? It'll only be a few dollars for you, but that's something."

Yes, he would like to do that, he said. So I called my friend as soon as he had left me and arranged it. Gregory and I would be over with a short ladder (which she said he would need) the next afternoon.

"And after you finish for her, Greg," I ventured, aware that I was on the edge of hassling, "how about helping your dad put up those heavy storm windows? It's time, now that it's November. His back is bothering him. I think he'd be glad of your help and he's done so much for you—" I waited uncertainly.

"I know. Okay. I'll help either Friday afternoon or Saturday morning. I don't work Saturdays, you know, and Ellen won't be back till afternoon."

So it was arranged. But the weekend didn't go as planned at all.

In the first place, Ellen returned on Friday quite unexpectedly. She was waiting at the front of the church in the U-Haul wagon when I started down the driveway to the rear entrance to pick up Gregory there. Astonished to see that apparition, I stopped my car halfway down. She blew her horn and waved to me. I got out and walked over to her.

Artie was with her. He was light colored, clean-shaven, cleanly dressed, about thirty years old. I liked his looks, shook hands with him, and took the opportunity to express my appreciation of the kindnesses he had shown my grandson. "He told me you were a good friend to him," I said, "and I'm always glad to meet his friends." He replied in a breathy voice, "He's a real nice boy."

"I think so, too. Someday you and he and Ellen must come to my apartment and have a cup of coffee with me so we can get better acquainted."

He nodded and I turned to Ellen. She waited for me to speak, her face impassive.

I said, "I don't think Gregory is looking for you today. He said you wouldn't be back till tomorrow. So he's planned to do a small piece of work, painting for a friend of mine."

"He told me to come today," she said quickly. "And we've—I've —got some plans made for this afternoon."

I said only, "I'm sorry. But this job won't take more than an hour. I really think he'll have to do that first, Ellen. My friend is staying at home on purpose waiting for us. And I've brought a ladder along —see! It's sticking through the back window of my car now. He's waiting down at the back and I'm sure—"

"Let me speak to him—*first,*" she broke in.

She was nettled. So was I a little. But I nodded agreeably. "Of course. I'll send him up to you. He must decide."

I drove on down to where Gregory was already waiting. He had not seen around the corner of the church and he was definitely surprised when I said Ellen was there, but he went up to speak to her as she had asked. I turned my car around and drove back up too, but stayed out of earshot. In the end, after about fifteen minutes of talking, he returned to me and we went to my friend's place. He did the work she had wanted done, while I waited, and then I drove him to Artie's, where Ellen had said she would wait. I did not drive directly there, as I had not yet been told exactly where the house was. I dropped him off at the monument again.

"I'll have to help Dad with the windows tomorrow," he said as he left me. "And, Gram, I didn't get paid today after all, even though it's Friday and my regular payday. Moe said he'll give it to me next week."

I nodded. "Thanks, darling, for helping my friend. She appreciated it. Shall I call Dad and tell him to wait till you come tomorrow morning? All right."

He did not come home to me that night. I was not surprised. It was Friday and Ellen was there. And he didn't like leaving her alone at Artie's. And my own vague words to him about bringing her here had conveyed no more to him than they had to me. So I wondered about Saturday. Would he even come then? Would Ellen perhaps go to her home again in the U-Haul? Was she paying for that too? Or was Artie? Or what? I thought how I had offered Gregory a home with me and he had said he wanted to come into it, but he wasn't doing that at all. Not really. His clothes hung in my closet. Food for him was in the fridge. But he was never there. It had been impossible to give him the regular meals I had planned on to build him up. He was really in worse shape now, it seemed to me, than when he had first come. What was the answer? The question haunted me.

So when he did not turn up at his father's house on Saturday morning when I went over there, I felt a flurry of anger. Ellen had taken control. Ellen had messed up everything. I had hoped and expected that helping his father would bridge over the chasm between him and Gregory.

Or was I being fair? Wasn't this the way Gregory was? Completely undependable? Never going where he had said he would go? Never doing what he had promised to do? Never remembering—or deliberately forgetting—I didn't know which. But he had *told* me he would do this, and he always kept his word to *me!* Always. Yes, this failure was Ellen's fault. She had distracted him somehow. *Ellen.* What about her? I had to decide something. I knew I wanted her for a friend, not an enemy. Because Ellen pulling one way and me pulling another would be no good. What must I do about her? What must I decide?

But before I did or decided anything, I had to find Gregory. I had to find him and make him help his father with those storm windows. I was right about this! I must make him see I was. It would be my first real battle with him—the other morning at breakfast had been only a skirmish—and I felt I had to win it.

So I drove down into the ghetto looking for Gregory that Saturday afternoon. Not knowing exactly where Artie lived or what his last name was, I had to stop and inquire of people. There were groups standing on the sidewalks everywhere. But I had no luck. Nobody knew any Artie. Nobody had ever heard of any Artie. Nobody knew of any Gregory either. "A tall thin white boy," I kept saying. But everybody only looked blankly or curiously at me. Me, a white woman alone in those narrow streets looking for a black man and a white boy—

Suddenly it came to me that I was doing just what Fern had always done. I was trying to make Gregory conform to *my* idea of what was right for him. I was *hassling*.

Overwhelmed by this realization and offering up thanks, in a rush, that I hadn't, after all, been able to find him—for wouldn't I have ruined everything if I had?—I went back to my apartment. If you never hassled, you accepted. That was it, in its simplest form. You accepted—and kept still. I had had a near miss.

Gregory did not, of course, return to me Saturday night, as I had been sure he wouldn't. And I was equally sure he wouldn't appear until very late on Sunday, so I had plenty of time both those nights to think. To think—and to remember.

4

And we know that all things work together for good to them that love God, to them who are the called according to his purpose.

Romans 8:28

Memories! So many came to me as I sat there alone and waiting—as usual. They explain, in part, the strong empathy that existed between Gregory and me. For he had shared his experiences with me of his own accord from the very beginning of my stay with Fern and her family. I had had the leisure to listen and I was a good listener. I did not interrupt and I was never shocked. Moreover I had no desire to turn what was told me into reproof or punishment. Such were Fern's and Tom's responsibilities.

There was the time when he came rushing up the stairs to my room crying out excitedly, "You can't guess where I've been, Gram! You can't *guess!* Wait till I tell you!" He was not thirteen then and he had gone, alone and fearless and against his parents' ruling, to New York, which city held a strange fascination for him. Knowing nothing about subways, he had yet managed to get himself to Times Square, where he had planned to see an adult movie forbidden at home. Refused admission because of his youth, he accosted an older person, a black, who was loitering nearby. Gregory, always democratic and impatient with any kind of social bars or distinctions, had offered to pay the entrance fee for both of them. After the show he accepted the man's invitation to his apartment and there, pretending he was accustomed to wine, he drank more than he could manage and found himself unable either to walk a straight line or remember the way to the subway station. Hearing all this in silence, my heart freezing with fear of what else might have happened, I awaited his next words. But he only said brightly— "He was a good guy, Gram. A real good guy. He went with me to the station and told me how my train was marked so I'd get on the right one. That's how I got back all right." He stopped, and I saw his brown eyes shining and his face alight with a wild triumphant joy as he finished— "I *did* it, Gram! I *did* it!" And I knew in that instant that he would have to go the whole long adventuresome way down the road he had that day chosen before he got to the end of it. How right I had been! And the end was not yet.

There was that memorable winter when he was in the eighth grade. He spent most of his time sitting in sullen idleness in the principal's office. It was I who went for him in the noon hour, since Fern, a teacher herself, was not free. Gregory loved fun and he had the gift of mimicry, and I can remember his saying, "It isn't fair, Gram! All I did was make the kids laugh." But daily he was dismissed from his class by his harassed teacher who called him "the best bad boy" in her room. The description pleased him. It gave him an aura of success, and it was the only thing he was best in, for he was a failure in all of his subjects. Not that he couldn't, Fern was told, but that he wouldn't. He refused even to try, as "none of the stuff was interesting." His failures, together with his cool ignoring of boundary lines and other established limitations at school, resulted in the request, in June, that Fern and Tom find a different educational setup for their son.

It was I who drove him in September to the place in New England finally selected for him, as Fern was in bed with pneumonia on the day he was to report. Our trip together was delightful. I was proud of him, of his looks, his manners, his charm—for he had a great deal. He was happy to be leaving his past and seemed to be anticipating his future, so when I left him it was with hope and confidence. But despite a successful adjustment to both classroom tasks and playing field rivalries, he was sent home in May for breaking the "no smoking" rule —and there was no alternative to a prompt dismissal.

Gregory—arriving with his suitcase filled with potent and expensive liquors which he had somehow obtained illegally. Gregory— laughing and strutting and feeling himself now an experienced man of the world. Gregory—showing no sense of guilt or remorse for what had happened but only a gay indifference and undampened high spirits. This shocked us all a little. He should have been dimmed, we felt. So, promptly an order of discipline was established, and tutoring to finish out the year's work was arranged. This filled the morning hours but the afternoons were free. Free and wild. In noisy old cars he and his friends, with whom he had quickly reestablished contact, careened about the countryside, crashed evening parties, went swimming in whatever pools took their fancy at any hour of the night, exchanged pornographic magazines, and drank and smoked on the distant parts of the golf club. Gregory was the leader, and being debonair, assured, and handsome, he was popular with both boys and girls.

When this began to pall, Gregory went further afield, drawn again into the city he found so fascinating. He usually went alone as he had before, and, alone, explored all that Greenwich Village had to offer. I only half believed his tales. But I listened just the same. He had tried new drinks and new drugs, had fought a few fights and attended secret mysterious meetings, had slept in pads with different girls each time. He had also learned to play cards, although not for money. He would come home with an expensive wristwatch or a high-priced camera or a good little radio and show them to me proudly. "I won these, Gram! But I'm not going to keep them. I'm going to sell them. It's the easiest way to earn money I know of. Much easier than holding down some stupid job." He had laughed. "I'll only work when my funds are low." I used to wonder about those winnings. Was he shoplifting? I did not know. But I was uneasy, and I worried about Gregory the rest of that summer.

Another memory—more reassuring. It was the night, long after midnight, when, hearing a noise downstairs, I went to investigate. In the kitchen I found Gregory with a girl about fourteen. She was crying and he was both scolding and comforting her. He introduced me and explained that he had spent the last two hours trying to persuade her not to run away from her home. For he knew, better than she, what would happen to her in the Village if she went. He had not been able to dissuade her, and as he hadn't wanted to leave her on the street corner at that hour, he had brought her to his house. He was going to cook them both some breakfast, he told me, and then he was going to sit there with her until she promised not to run away but go back to her own home. When she did, he would take her.

And he did. Because she did.

The only predictable thing about Gregory was his unpredictability. But I was happy to discover that beneath his wild ways there lay a warm, kind thoughtfulness.

Then there was the afternoon I towed Gregory's jalopy from the yard where he had bought it with an unexpected windfall of money from a recent birthday. Telling me of his wonderful find, he had said, "It's great, Gram! The only thing is the motor doesn't run and I don't know how I'll get it home." I promptly made an offer and he leaped at it. "Gram! *Could* you—*would* you, really? Is your Chevy *strong* enough to pull it?" I could and I would and it was. So, with him proudly at the wheel of his purchase, I dragged it behind me across the railroad tracks, around corners and down the quietest streets until we reached his driveway. What a friend I was to him that day!

Three weeks later he and the two friends who had helped him get the car into some kind of running condition took off for California in it. They departed secretly on a moonless night late in August, with only a bill of sale to prove it was not stolen, without a registration card or a driver's license or a spare tire or money or anything of any value except a gold signet ring which I had given Gregory the preceding Christmas. They managed breakfasts by stealing milk and rolls from back porches early in the morning. And they earned two dinners by waiting on customers at a drive-in restaurant. But the motor kept breaking down, and when finally Gregory could no longer fix it—and the shops and garages were all closed because it was midnight—and they had no money—and it was cold and pouring down rain—and they had had nothing to eat for ten hours—they huddled down to wait shivering in the back seat for somebody to come rescue them. Help came in the form of a police patrol car. The officer arrested them as minors and vagrants and took them to the station nearest to Atlantic City, where he telephoned the parents to come get them. When Gregory, home again, had been fed and had had a shower, he came into my room to give me the details of his trip. "Only bad thing was—I had to pawn the ring you gave me, Gram. I had to do it. But I kept

the pawn ticket, and on the way back Dad stopped at the shop and
went in and got it back for me. I thought you wouldn't like it if I didn't
have it. See! Here it is." That was when I really understood how well
I stood with him.

Up to now Gregory's escapades had been the usual normal ones of
childhood and adolescence and so not to be viewed too seriously. But
inevitably in due course he got himself into real trouble. I think the
following incident happened *before* the attempt to go to California,
but I am not sure.

It was quite late on a moonlit night when he and his companion,
heading for home after a drinking party, came upon an old graveyard
lying peacefully in a quiet whiteness. Pausing, they looked at the
ancient tombstones set at crazy precarious angles, and the same
thought came to them simultaneously. Fun! There it was. In a moment they were running up and down the overgrown paths, giving a
push here, a shove there, and laughing softly at the quiet thump of
stone on sod or the crumbling crash of broken fragments—when
suddenly a policeman loomed up beside them.

The affair was written up in the local paper, the townspeople everywhere were horrified at the desecration, and the church brought suit
for wanton destruction of property. Tom, of course, had had to engage
a lawyer, who was able to arrange private conferences so neither boy
had to appear in court. Furthermore, he was a man who understood
boys. He spoke their language, and Gregory opened up to him freely.
I was present at one conference, as Fern had had to attend a teachers'
meeting out of town. I can remember almost verbatim what Gregory
said that afternoon.

Why! He hadn't dreamed there was any value in those old stones!
He was surprised anyone cared anything about them. Sure, he knew
right from wrong. But that hadn't seemed wrong to him because he'd
never thought the graveyard belonged to anyone special. It was just
there. Like a brook or something. Sort of forgotten, as if nobody ever
went there. How was he to know people did? It could have been a
place to play, he thought. Sure, he believed in God. Only he'd never
thought about God's being in a place like that, *outside* a church! But,
sure, there was a God all right—because who else had made the sun
and the moon and the stars? And, sure, he was sorry and sure, he'd

help pay for the damage. He'd get a job. He had one right then, as a matter of fact, helping a gardener. How much would he—*five thousand dollars!* Wow! That couldn't be right! For those old broken stones? Wow! But—sure, he'd try to pay it—he and his friend. But he'd be an old man before he got *that* paid off. A real old man. He couldn't even *imagine* how much five thousand dollars was—

Yes, he'd been younger then. This must have been before he went to the school in New England— And then my thoughts moved on to the second school that had been tried.

This school was on Long Island and chosen by Fern because its rules about smoking were lenient. Other rules were lenient, too. So we were hopeful. But his career there ended just before Christmas when he and another boy, sneaking out of their dormitory one midnight, stole a car which Gregory drove without a license and quite thoroughly demolished against a tree. He himself was uninjured and his companion suffered only a mild concussion.

Fern and Tom, to whom the school telephoned around one o'clock in the morning, left very early that day to drive down for their son and, with him, face the consequences. They found him, white and weary, at the principal's office, with a police guard at the door. The story of the accident was told and retold, with Gregory denying nothing, and after a time two more policemen drove them all to the courthouse, where charges were entered and a time set in the future for the arraignment and—later still—the trial. I was giving Bruce his supper when Gregory came in behind his parents that night, silent and subdued after a longer day than he had ever known.

This first brush with the formalities of the law brought a marked change in him. Up to then he had been laughingly scornful of rules and regulations. Beating them was a game. You could get away with anything, because the police were stupid and you were smart. Never before had he been forced to go through the routine of appearing in court. That day he saw nowhere around him anyone that he knew. Only strangers, unfriendly and in uniform. In a kind of daze he heard that he was now a juvenile delinquent and as such was on probation. He heard what that meant. It meant that he was no longer free. A probation officer would be assigned to him to whom he must report weekly. He could not associate in the future with any boys he knew who were on probation like himself. He must get a job after school hours. He must be in his own home by ten o'clock at night and he must never—*never*—leave the town where he lived without getting permission both from his parents and his probation officer.

All this he heard in the huge, cold, echoing courtroom. And the white-haired judge in his black gown, with his slow, deep, solemn tones, had been impressive and awesome. For the first time Gregory was frightened. He had left that scene knowing a sentence hung over him which he would not be told about for a number of weeks. The days that followed, with this hovering uncertainty, this suspenseful weight of fear, this unknown and unguessed future (he would be sent away somewhere—but where? and for how long?) unnerved him—and we saw him, to our great surprise and consternation, go into a deep retreat within himself.

Never shall I forget that time.

Through the day he kept closely to his room with the shades drawn down, and at night he would burn only one small red bulb in the ceiling globe, which gave an eerie and depressing effect. Nor would he go out to mingle with his friends, even those still permitted him. But worst of all was the fact that he could not sleep. He would creep downstairs after everyone had retired to sit for hours before the television box, watching anything that came on the screen. This change in him was alarming. It was during this period, before judgment had been given and shortly after the accident, that the rapport with this grandson of mine was immeasurably strengthened.

Aware that he was not sleeping and that he left his bed to sit alone before the TV set, I used to join him. We sat for hours together, saying nothing or very little and only of what we were watching. Once I asked him if he minded my presence and he said, "No. I like it. It's not so lonely." So I stayed. Finally in the early morning hours I would get him a cup of hot chocolate or a glass of milk and a sandwich and would ask him if now he didn't feel he could go up and sleep. It was almost daylight then, so he would agree and we would part. I never knew what his thoughts were at that time, but I tried to convey to him that I shared his anguish and that I still loved him. I hoped this would be comforting.

In the end he was not sent away anywhere. I was glad. I felt Gregory had been badly damaged and needed the warm understanding love and protection of his home. We offered it—but he held us off. And though he emerged gradually from the shell into which he had retreated, he was different. Without demur he accepted the imposed limitations. Without argument or anger he listened to his parents' advice and admonitions—but then with stony face, he walked away in silence. He would discuss nothing. We were strangers to him, and he to us. And though he seemed to have made an adjustment to life again, it was only a shield, a cloak around him to hide his real feelings. And what these were, I felt I knew. I thought he was being bolstered to a new confidence, perhaps a dangerous confidence, by his pride in the prominence he had achieved through his misdeeds, and by the admiration of his peers, to whom he had become something of a hero. This was a confusion of values that troubled me, and I wanted to talk to him about it. But he was closed even to me. I could not reach him. He had forgotten—or did not wish to remember—the vigils we had shared together. He wanted to forget that dependence he had had on me, for he had decided to stand alone. So he was impenetrable, and all I could do was ache for him.

That is one of my bitterest memories.

Another was only a little less poignant. He came into the house one bitter cold night that winter with a small mongrel pup in his arms, wrapped in his own coat. Fern, seeing him without it on, exclaimed, "Gregory! What on earth—" But he interrupted her.

"I didn't need it. But the dog did. There was a litter and nobody wanted this one. So I took him. I want to keep him."

The compassion I have always felt for Gregory was the greater because he could not, apparently, love anyone back. Except that small white pup. How he did love that little animal! I have a snapshot of him holding the dog in his arms as he sits on the stairs of his home. And there is on his face a look of sadness I had never seen before. It shows an unmistakable wistfulness for something lost or something not yet found. There, I have always told myself, is the real Gregory.

But how to reach him? In the distance between us then, I found myself as surprised as Fern when he ran away a second time.

He went because he hated the world. He hated the town in which he lived and he hated everybody in it. Especially the policemen who were always watching him even if he was only standing still in the depot park. They watched him, and then they came up to him to ask him what he was doing there and where he was going, and then they would tell him to move on. When he was doing *nothing.* And he also and particularly hated his parents, who were both against him, forever arguing with him, and explaining to him why he should or shouldn't do this or that. Trying to change him, when he liked himself because he was smarter than they were. Trying to make him go to church too. Why should he? What did church have besides hymns and hypocrites? He hated church most of all, maybe, because of that graveyard mess. He'd never finished paying for it. And now there was the car he'd smashed to pieces down on Long Island—and a lawyer for *that.* It was all too much.

I knew that was why he went. But by the time I knew it he was gone. And Fern had found the labels which he had ripped from his clothes and dropped in the wastebasket. So it was clear to us that he didn't want to be found.

At that moment my chimes sounded and my glance flew to the clock. Almost midnight. This Sunday evening at an end—and my waiting too. For that must be Gregory. I hurried to let him in.

5

If ye have faith as a grain of mustard seed, ye shall say unto this mountain, Remove hence to yonder place; and it shall remove; and nothing shall be impossible unto you.

Matthew 17:20

He staggered in, looking absolutely exhausted. His face, the ruddy color of his youth wiped away, was pale and closed. His eyes met mine blankly. He spoke my name, nodded that he would eat something, and in the kitchen he sank down in a chair where he stayed, silent and immovable, slumped in an attitude of unutterable weariness. At last, after a little food and some coffee, he spoke, his words coming heavily.

His throat was sore, he said, and his neck stiff. Outside it was cold and raw and raining and he'd been out in that weather all day and up until this moment. Yesterday, too. He'd been moving a couple of people Artie knew into another house. But because the U-Haul was a small one and wouldn't hold much, it had taken much longer than he'd expected. It had taken all these past two days, which was why he hadn't gone to help his father with those storm windows. Anyway, he'd made twenty dollars and that had helped pay the rental of the truck. Tonight he'd returned it, and Artie was going to take Ellen back to her house in his car. "That's why I'm here," he finished.

Before I could say anything, he went on, in the same dead way.

"I don't think I'll be able to work at the church tomorrow, Gram. I don't feel good. I ache all over. Anyway, I think I'm going to quit there. I've got another job I can take that'll pay better. About twice as much. I can drive a garbage truck for Edgewood. I talked to the boss about it tonight. He wants me. I can start tomorrow if I like. Or any time."

A garbage truck. His grandfather, who had been a successful publisher in New York and the mayor in our town, would turn over in his grave. His grandmother, the social arbiter here, would rise up too. But I said nothing. He went on.

"I'm not proud, Gram. I'll do that. It's much better pay. The only thing is I'll have to be down there at five thirty in the morning."

"Gregory," I said quietly. "Will you please do a little *thinking?* How are you going to wake up at five-thirty in the morning when it's all I can do to get you up at eight-thirty? You would have to be out of bed as early as five, as a matter of fact, in order to get down there by five-thirty. And how will you get there? There'll be no bus running at that hour. And nobody on the road to give you a hitch. Do you think *I'm* going to rout you out and drive you to that job at that time of day?"

"No, of course not, Gram."

"Think, Greg. You never *think.* You go off the deep end without thinking or looking. Don't you realize you'll have to go back to live at Artie's if you take that job? You can't live here and make it on time. You know that!"

Silence. I pushed what I thought might be an advantage.

"Besides, it's outdoor work. In all kinds of weather. And you've said to me you are glad you can be inside the church because you don't like the cold. You have a sore throat now. But if you have that job you'll have to go out, sore throat or not, every day. It's up to you, Gregory, what you do. I'm not telling you, darling. I'm just asking you to look at all sides of the question before you give up the church work. Personally, I'll miss you very much if you leave me. But it's up to you."

"It's the money, Gram."

"I know. I understand. But we'll keep trying for an afternoon job for you."

So we left it and he went to bed. As did I. But not to sleep. Gregory was like a storm-tossed ship at sea, I thought. Without a compass. Without a chart. Without sails or even oars. Indeed, without any direction or destination. And without even an anchor to drop until he found where he wanted to go. I had thrown him an anchor. Was he going to pull it up and drift on helplessly now over turbulent waves that gave him no rest? No. I could not sleep.

In the morning—Monday—it was impossible to get Gregory awake. *Really* impossible. He simply groaned and said he was too sick to go to the church today. I would have to telephone Moe that he could not get there. He would go later if he felt better. All thought of driving the garbage truck had apparently been forgotten.

There was no use in arguing with him. There never was. Besides, that would be hassling. However, since this was his first time to default, perhaps Moe would be forgiving. I telephoned to the church and asked the business manager there to relay the message to Moe.

"Gregory is ill," I said. "It sounds like a touch of the flu. He has a sore throat and he aches all over. He isn't able to work for Moe today."

"If he's ill, it's just as well he's not coming," was the reply, "for our furnace is out of order and we are getting no heat. Tell him to stay home all day."

I thanked him, and, relieved, I reported this to Gregory.

He slept all the morning. By noon he felt a little better. By noon I had come to a decision, and while he was eating a belated breakfast I told him of it.

"Greg darling," I began, "this way of living is no good. You're here but you're not here. Tell me something. Are you and Ellen planning to get married?"

"No," he said. "We've given up that idea. Her folks don't like me. Her father says he'll throw her out if she marries me. Anyway, we've decided against it. We don't believe in it. We don't think getting married is necessary. We just want to be together, that's all. We *need* each other, Gram." He paused. "We've got problems."

"Yes. Well, then, I think you'd better be together here rather than down at Artie's. You're trying to live in two places at once and you can't do it. Tell Ellen if she wants to come here, I will welcome her."

"You said that before."

"And now I'm saying it again."

He looked at me for a long moment, puzzled, uncertain. Then— "Where would she sleep?"

"There are two beds in my room, you know."

"She won't like that,"—quickly.

"Neither will I."

There was a silence, pregnant with our unspoken thoughts. Finally he said, slowly, "We *need* each other, Gram. I told you."

"I remember. I understand."

There it was. What was he going to make out of it? I waited. His face told me little although his eyes held a hard, frustrated anger. Presently he shrugged and got to his feet. "Mom said she'd do my laundry for me. I'll take it to her." And he went out.

Had he given me an answer? I did not know. *"You'll have Ellen on your neck,"* Fern had said. Now she would say I was out of my mind. She would say my idea was impossible. But nothing was impossible! I had learned that you could always do what seemed right and necessary. And that was how this now appeared to me.

For I had offered Gregory a home and he had taken me up on my offer. So far it hadn't worked out well. But that didn't mean it couldn't. That didn't mean we had reached an end. Weren't we really just at the beginning? A *new* beginning. A beginning I would indeed not like, for my age required the dignity of privacy. But I had set out to help my grandson—and I still wanted to, for I still loved him. And if having him here meant having Ellen too— Well, what choice had I? I could not bear the thought of the higgledy-piggledy life he was leading. I could not bear the thought of his going back to Artie's. I could not bear the thought, either, of my giving up so soon. We could start fresh. So then, this was something that had to be. That was all. It simply had to be. If he wanted it. If he and Ellen both wanted it.

If! Again—*if.*

6

Behold, O Lord; for I am in distress. . . .

Lamentations 1:20

I was not surprised when Gregory did not return to me that afternoon from Fern's. I had given him something to think about and he
would have to talk it over with Ellen. If she was at Artie's he would
go there. I had the faint hope but no real expectation of their appearing some time this evening. That is, if she did not turn down my offer
cold. How badly pressed was she for money? Perhaps the car was
costing her more than she had expected. And of course she had to pay
her father— How much would her unemployment check cover? Was
it because it wouldn't cover everything that Gregory had felt he must
turn garbage collector? I felt they were both desperate.

Earlier in the day, when he had finally dressed and eaten and the
rain had stopped, he had said he might go to the church to pick up
from Moe the paycheck he had not been given last Friday. Then (he
had said) he could pay me the five dollars we had agreed upon for his
board. Whether he had gone there before taking his laundry to Fern
I didn't know. But it didn't matter. The money was of no importance
except that meeting this obligation—and it had been his own idea—
would, I had thought, increase his self-respect.

Well (my thoughts went on) let him come any time he chooses. He
has a key. I gave him one last week. And let him bring Ellen or not.
He must decide.

Presently the day waned and darkness came. Getting my own
supper I recalled my earlier resolution to give Gregory good meals
regularly. I was going to build him up—and what had happened? He
had been with me for just two breakfasts, no lunches, and not yet for
any dinners. Half of the time he didn't eat his snack, he had admitted,

and what could I say or do about that? Nothing. Exactly nothing. Unless I wanted to hassle him. What I had undertaken to do, I thought, was not easy.

And now I had before me one more long evening of restlessness and uncertainty. Would it continue to be this way? If so, would I get used to it? Or—if Ellen came—would we be able to establish some order in our daily lives? Only one thing was clear to me. I would not play policewoman. There must be a sense of freedom for all of us. I did not go beyond that. I simply knew that this was essential and the one way we could manage the close proximity I had suggested. It was not for me to live their lives for them or instruct them in living their own. It was only for me to remember that there was a great gap between eighteen and eighty, and the burden of the understanding which might bridge that gap would rest on me because I had the longest view. I must, therefore, be generous in my judgment—perhaps, indeed, withhold it.

It was morning and Gregory had not come home. Was this his answer? Would he never return again? I could not guess and I was heavyhearted, because not knowing is worse than knowing. I worried too about whether he would get to his job at the church on time. He could easily be late. And Moe wouldn't stand for that, especially as Gregory had missed all day yesterday. I considered telephoning to Fern to ask her how he had acted when he was there, to find out what he might have said that would give me a hint of his feelings then or his plans. But I decided against this for it would only alarm her. And I wasn't ready, anyway, to speak of the offer I had made.

What I could do, of course, was drive for the third time to the monument to see if he was there or on his way. Action would give me relief. But would he think this was hassling? He hadn't thought so before. Anyway, I had to go. I couldn't bring myself to call the church. It was too much like spying. Too much an admission. So thinking, I went quickly out to my car. All along the way my eyes went searching on both sides of the street for a familiar figure. But it was not to be seen. Nor was Gregory at the monument either when I reached it. And suddenly then I grew cold with fear.

But I would not admit it. I would not give it room. He could be late, I told myself. I would just wait and see. He would come loping along soon. So I circled the monument and found a parking place along the curb and sat there, twisting my head around every few minutes to see if he was coming. I waited that way for fifteen minutes by my watch. It was nine o'clock now. Even so, I waited for fifteen minutes more. But no Gregory appeared. Reaching for hope and comfort, I said to myself that this time he had really hitchhiked with somebody. He was probably already at the church. Had indeed reached it before I had left my apartment. Yes, that was it! Well, I would go find out. With a quick indrawn breath, I started my motor. I had to bring an end to this suspense.

I saw Moe as I turned down the driveway to the rear entrance. He was lame and was having a slow and laborious time hauling out to the playground below all the heavy children's equipment from the shelter where it was kept. This was Gregory's main job.

I stopped my car and called out, "Where's Gregory?"

He limped over to me. I could see he was angry and, as always, outspoken. "That's what I want to know. He's not here. And I'm going to have to tell you I can't keep him any longer. He's no good, Mrs. Randall. He's just no help at all. And I can't put up with his ways any longer. I've had it. Don't *you* know where he is?"

I shook my head. "No. He didn't come back to me last night. I was sure I'd find him here, Moe. He wants this job. He needs it." My voice held a pleading note. I was outwardly calm but I was rigid with unbelief. What ever had happened? Had I made a dreadful—a fatal —mistake last night about Ellen?

Moe came closer. "I see you bringing him here every day—and coming for him—and it makes me mad. He's no good," he repeated. "He's on drugs. He's been on them for a long time is my guess. He's a real sick boy. He's not what he used to be when he was a kid and I gave him his first job here. Then he was all right. On his toes. Eager. Interested. Now he's *sick,* I tell you. And he don't care. He's on speed. Or LSD. Or heroin. Or maybe all three. I don't know. But he's not worth shucks to me. He can't remember what I tell him to do ten minutes. He's always asking me what I said. Over and over I say it. And he falls asleep. I've got a couch in my office, and when I can't find him at work doin' what he's supposed to be doin', well—there he is. Asleep on my couch. I hate to tell you all this, Mrs. Randall, but you should know, if you don't. I thought maybe you did and just didn't want to let on 'cause you kept on hopin'. Well, you're wastin' your time. And he's wastin' mine. So I can't keep him anymore. I've told the business manager I can't. I gave him a try like I was asked to do, but I've got to have a boy I can depend on. This work here now. Getting out all this stuff. It's too much for me. I'm sorry. But that's how it is."

I heard him to the end. All along I had felt there might be more wrong than I knew—but I had, as Moe said, hoped. I had pushed troublesome anxiety way to the back of my mind. I gave it no room. But never once had it occurred to me that Gregory couldn't physically do his work. I had worried about promptness and whether he and Moe would get along together—but for him to fall *asleep*— I straightened my shoulders and answered Moe quietly.

"Thank you for telling me all this, Moe. Yes, I should know. And I'm sorry you had to be the one to tell me. It was hard for you. I just want you to know I understand that—and how you feel about not keeping Gregory any longer. If you want to get another boy to take his place—go ahead. You need someone. And thanks for giving him a trial, anyway. By the way, haven't you a last check for him? I'll take it if you have. Or did he come for it yesterday?"

"Yesterday! He was sick yesterday. I gave it to him last *Friday.* He told me he needed it, and it was his payday so I gave it to him. Did he say I didn't?"

I nodded. He shook his head.

"Mrs. Randall, he's no good. Don't bother about him anymore. I know you love him. He's your grandson. But he's not worth your worry."

I nodded again and left him to drive back to my empty apartment. I came into it feeling numb all over. Most of what Moe had said was true and I knew it. That was the worst of it all. I *knew* it. But such things had never been said to me by any outsider before. Fern might speak with such frankness but no one else. Yet his words—"He's not worth your worry"—I could not forget. They kept repeating themselves over and over in my head. Was that true—really? In the frozen silence that held me I now asked myself another question: Had I stopped loving my grandson because I had learned some ugly truths about him? I sank with a kind of helplessness into my wing chair.

How long I sat there in a blank state I don't remember. But after a while I got up slowly and went to open the closet door behind which all Gregory's clothes hung. There they were. Put there by me only a week ago in such relief and thankfulness. Gregory wanted to live with me! It had been his choice, his decision, because he could get along with me better than with his parents. Where they had failed, I had thought I would be successful.

That was what I had thought. That was what I had hoped. That was what I had believed.

But I had been wrong, and with that recognition the ground had now dropped away completely from under me. For Gregory, after only a short few days with me, had left me. Without a word. Without any explanation. Without any thanks. The undertaking had been a complete failure. Gregory knew I loved him. But he had thrown this love right back in my face. Even though I had offered Ellen a home with me too. And in leaving he had lied to me. Somehow that was worse than finding out he was on drugs.

I was as cold as a stone, thinking these things. I could feel nothing. Not anger. Not even regret. Or a faint flickering hope that somehow I was mistaken. That somehow everything could be explained away. No. I felt nothing at all. I was simply stunned, empty of all emotion. After only a week, to have this happen! I had thought the week had gone well. We had had no words, no ugliness of any kind. That was the thing! It shouldn't have happened without some *reason!* There had *been* no reason. Unless it was about my asking Ellen— But we could have talked that over. We should have. This should never have happened. Not so *soon.*

However, it had happened. And there was nothing to do but believe it. Gregory wasn't here. He had left me. And he had quit his job. And he had lied to me. So now what?

Slowly I reached out my hand and began to take Gregory's clothes out of the closet. There was a laundry bag hanging there and I lifted it down and started putting his things in it. His heavy sweater and two thick shirts first. Underwear next. Then a pair of pants carefully folded. Then his rolls of sox and a small leather case for his personal toilet articles on top. There wasn't room for everything so I brought a large paper bag from the kitchen and put the rest in that. His shoes —his boots—they must go loose in the car. I watched myself doing all this as though I were another person. When I had finished I went to the telephone and called Fern.

"Fern? I'm bringing all Gregory's clothes—everything he owns—back to you."

"Mother! What's happened?"

"I don't know. He's not here. I don't know where he is. He's not at the church, either. Nothing's worked out, that's all. So it's all over."

"Mother, don't feel too badly. I thought it would turn out this way."

"I didn't. But it has. And I'm sorry. The thing is—I can't go on. I'll be over with his things soon. They're all packed. I'm going to put them in the car now. I'll be right over." And I hung up.

I was still numb. I couldn't even feel sorry although I had said I was. I still felt nothing at all. I was frozen. Gregory had let me down. *Me.* When I loved him so much and he knew it. *Love is not enough.* That was what our minister had said. What was, then? What *was?*

Before I went to my daughter's with Gregory's possessions—his little radio too—I mustn't forget that—I called the superintendent of our apartment house and asked him to come over for a moment as I had to speak to him about something important that couldn't wait.

To him I said, "I've had my grandson living here with me, as you know. Did I tell you he is a drug addict? I wasn't sure—but now I'm positive. And he's not to be trusted. So I don't want him here with me anymore. Unfortunately, I gave him a key. Now I would like to have you change the lock on my door and give me another set of keys. I don't feel comfortable knowing he and his friends can get in here at any time. Will you take care of that for me right away, please?"

He did. He was sympathetic and understanding. He had sons of his own and one of them worried him sometimes too. I thanked him when he had finished, gave him a generous tip and said, "Even if Gregory comes to you and asks you to let him in, don't do it. He may say I sent him to ask this of you. But it won't be true. He's a liar, you know. So just don't ever let him in."

I heard myself saying all these things and still I felt nothing. Then I went to Fern's house with Gregory's clothes. She carried everything in and put it in a corner of the kitchen.

"I've got a lot of food I bought for him. I'll never eat it all."

"I'll come for it tomorrow—if you really don't want to keep it." She put her arms around me. "Don't feel so badly. I'm not surprised, you know. Tom won't be surprised. Nobody can live with Gregory. Nobody. He won't take any help. I don't know what's going to happen to him. But I don't believe he'll come back to us even though he has a key and knows he can. Thanks for trying, Mother."

Back in my apartment I sat down to think what next.

I had time to think. The place was very quiet. Gregory was not there and would never come back. Or would he? Suddenly I realized he might. Perhaps tonight he would put in an appearance, bringing Ellen and some excuse for his behavior. But I had had enough. I didn't want to see him or hear anything he might say. It would be a lie. He'd lied to me about his paycheck. He could lie again. I no longer believed in him at all. All right, then. I would put a note out for him to read if he should come back. He would read it and go away and that would be the end. The end of a hope—a belief—a dream.

I wrote the note. It was brief and bleak. It said only—"Gregory: I'm sorry your stay with me didn't work out. You have a key to your dad's house. You will have to go there. I've taken all your clothes over. Gram."

I folded it, wrote his name on the envelope and fastened it with Scotch tape to the outside of my vestibule door. When the key he had wouldn't unlock it—if he came—he would see the note and would read it. I would not hear him if he called to me. I would not let him in. It was all over between us.

I sat there at my desk—thinking—remembering. How many notes had I written to him through the years? Hundreds! And they had always begun "Gregory darling" and they had always ended "Love, Gram." But not this time. Not this one.

My mind traveled back again into the past.

When he had run away the second time, hating everything and everybody, I could not write him, for we did not know where he had gone. And we did not try to find out, on the advice of our lawyer, who was sure Gregory would return when his money gave out and he was hungry enough. But it was almost four months before he reappeared—unannounced and in the company of two older boys who had a car with Tennessee license plates. Fern welcomed them all, fed them a dinner, and provided sleeping quarters on the third floor for the strangers.

The suitcase he had brought home did not, as before, contain potent drinks, but only clothes, scattered through which were dozens of torn, crumpled scraps of paper on which were penciled telephone numbers, names, and addresses of people scattered all over the whole country. His explanation—too vague, too fluent, yet too garbled—about the musical group they were, with performance dates all the way to the West Coast, did not in the least satisfy Fern. She suspected a connection with a ring of drug pushers, and she and Tom took all the questionable evidence to the police station, leaving action, if considered necessary, to the chief. As a result, Gregory was arrested early the next morning on charges of breaking his probation and leaving the town without permission. He was taken—being only sixteen and too young for jail—to the children's shelter for a month of observation, questioning, and testing. The other two boys, possessing nothing incriminating, were sent on their way. Gregory accompanied the police officer quietly and without apparent surprise.

After he was released he came to see me in the apartment to which I had moved in his absence and, once again, talked to me freely. He told me of thumbing rides all the way to the mecca where he had friends waiting. Of how he had enrolled in the university down there as a student, thus being entitled to free meals as well as free tuition. How he had lived with a senior, and how he had made money by selling the notes he took in his classes to students unwilling to attend the lectures themselves. And he told me also of his exploring the city.

He had gone to museums and musicals and concerts in the park. To séances and hypnotism classes, to churches of all creeds, as well as to meetings of private religious cults where he had learned about Satan and black magic and witchcraft. But the best of all was the business he had set up which was so successful he could buy new clothes, rent a car, and even fly once to California. I interrupted for the first time I could remember to ask a question. What was this business? But he had grown cautious then, and his too careful reply made me aware that he had become cognizant of the strong tides of evil in the world. Evil that was much more than juvenile mischief, that held danger, and that had somehow informed him of the power of the Mafia. And it flashed to my mind that perhaps the reason he had been so docile when he had been arrested was that whatever he had been doing with all those names and addresses and telephone numbers had grown out of hand, and the safety promised by a month at the shelter was surer than any promise that might have been connected with the Mafia. I could hardly credit this, but it seemed a possibility. Anyway, his experience—all of it—had not lessened his desire to do more, know more, dare more, whatever the risks. He still felt that he could swim against whatever tides he might encounter and could conquer life on his own terms. However, he seemed at the same time willing to postpone any further adventure at the moment. He was free, safe, and home—and it all seemed good to him. He would stay awhile, he said, because he had plans that he thought would surprise me—"and please you too, Gram."

They did. He had decided to enroll in a government-run school where, after a few weeks of study, he could get a high-school-equivalency diploma—if he passed the final tests. "And I will pass, Gram. I'm going to. I've made up my mind." And he did. It was one of the high points of his life and I shared it with him, for it was I who drove him to the university along the river where he had to take his examinations. So I saw him when he emerged after two hours and walked toward my car with his easy arrogant grace and said, in an exultant low voice, "I've *got* it, Gram! I've *got* it!"

With a high-school diploma and a driver's license, which had been his next reach for manhood, he seemed a changed person. All his earlier *joie de vivre* had returned, and his plans to repay his father, who had undertaken to settle Gregory's debts for him in his absence, exhibited a new maturity that lifted our hearts. Gregory was two people and had been at war with himself during the past years, but now the war was over.

We were too hasty in our thinking. Gregory was still two people. And one of these was the impatient youth we thought he had outgrown. He wasn't earning enough money at his stupid job of driving a truck around town! He wasn't going to go on dragging along at this rate! He would never get out of debt unless he found a quicker way to pay it off! Well, he'd learned a quicker way in the South. It would work here, too. Within only a few weeks after getting his diploma he was involved in secret meetings with the juvenile delinquents he had known earlier. They gathered at Gregory's house when Fern was not there. At those times they posted one of themselves as a guard so they would not be surprised at her return. I encountered this guard once. Fern had asked me to find out what was going on—if I could. She had always leaned on me because of my closeness to Gregory. So I went to their house and asked the guard to send my grandson out to speak with me for a moment. He came. But he was tense and nervous and completely uncommunicative. He had a cigarette in his hand. "It's marijuana," he said defiantly. He had been drinking too. And the drinking along with the smoking was changing him into the quarrelsome and ungovernable person with whom nothing could be done. He began ignoring the limitations still imposed on him. He came in at night when he pleased. He failed to report to his probation officer. He wasn't turning up for his meals. All this I had hoped to talk about, but I was turned away with an impatience unusual from him to me. He was plainly resolved to remain distant, and within a few moments he said, "Gram, I'm very busy right now. I'll have to ask you to leave." So I did.

Only a few days later Gregory was arrested for some misdemeanor connected with his driving. He had exceeded the speed limit. He had parked by a fire hydrant. He had ignored a stop signal. And this time he was old enough for jail. But, perhaps because the charges were minor, he was sent to a state reformatory where a regimen of group therapy was having rather successful results with refractory boys like Gregory. It was then I began writing to him again. Long letters—two a week—urging him to accept the therapy, not fight it, because I was sure that, deep down, he was really ashamed and unhappy in the web of deceit and trickery in which he had again enmeshed himself. So I wrote—

Sharply I pulled myself back to the present moment. This note I had put on my door was the last one I would ever write him. And this was not signed, "Love, Gram."

I read again what I had written and left it there. That brief, bleak note remained on my door all through that night, and Gregory did not appear to read it. I left it on a second night and still he did not appear. On the following morning—Thursday—as I sat at my kitchen table over my coffee, thought stirred in me, if not emotion. And I said to myself, Maybe I'm wrong. Maybe something serious has happened to him and he really couldn't—can't—come back. How do I know? He lives in the ghetto and he carries an ugly knife and he is taking drugs now— Yet if anything had indeed happened, wouldn't I have learned of it by now? Wouldn't something have been written up in the local daily paper? But I had seen nothing.

I thought further. I could word that letter differently. It need not be as harsh as it is. As unforgiving and cruel. If he should come back —if anything had actually gone wrong for him and he came back needing me, really in trouble with no one else to turn to—and he read that note and discovered I wouldn't help him, that I had pushed him out of my life— oh! I was uneasy.

I rose from the table. I had decided I would write another note. I moved quickly out to my living room and opened my front door. There was that note still. Lifting my hand, I tore it off and then went to my desk to try and work out something different. Something gentler. I was about to sit down when my telephone rang in the kitchen and I went to answer it first.

"Gram?"

Could I believe my ears? I was still empty, still drained, but at the sound of that voice I caught my breath, and then feeling flooded back and I could hardly speak. Over my pounding heart I heard my shaking voice.

"Greg! Where *are* you?"

"I'm at the church, Gram."

"At the *church!* What—what are you doing at the church?"

"I'm working. I've been working here all the morning. Moe took me back. When I explained everything he took me back. Gram! I want to *tell* you where I've been these last two or three days! I want to *tell* you!"

My heart was flooded with an unbearable joy. I put my head down on my arms and spoke aloud in a shaking voice. "Oh, thank You, God! Thank You!"

7

His words poured out while I, my mind dizzy with relief and joy, tried to follow.

"I decided—all of a sudden—to give up drugs, Gram. I've been thinking about it quite a while, but I decided suddenly last weekend when I didn't come home. So I went to the council in Edgewood that's set up for boys who need help and they gave me some advice. They sent me to the clinic in Milltown where they have what is called a *detox* program. I had to go there every day to see doctors and take tests and meet with the people who run the place, and that's what I've been doing. I've hitchhiked over in the morning to get there when it opened and I've been there all day. But now I'm *in!* I'm accepted. I'm to start on the methadone tomorrow after one more conference today, and that's why I'm calling you, Gram. Can you take me over when I finish here for Moe? He took me back, like I said, after I showed him all the doctors' appointment cards I had. He believed me and took me back. But I have this one more appointment this afternoon and I'm afraid if I try to hitch I'll be late. So—can you?"

I found my very shaky voice. "Gregory darling, that's the best news I've ever had. Of course I'll take you over. Have you told your mother?"

"Yes. She just happened to come here for a meeting or something, so I told her."

Remembrance came to me suddenly. How would *I* tell him what *I* had done? "Gregory, listen. I have some news, too. I took all your clothes back to your mother's house yesterday."

"Gram! You *did!* You *didn't!* Why did you do that?" He was shocked.

56

"Well, you didn't appear here. And you didn't telephone. So I thought I must have hassled you somehow and you didn't want to live with me anymore. Or else you had decided to drive that garbage truck and were going to stay at Artie's again so you'd be there early in the morning. How was I to know, darling?"

"But—Gram! *Can't* I come back to you?"

"Is that what you want?"

"Yes! I want to live with *you.*"

"Then you shall. I'll go get your clothes and bring them all back here today while you're in Milltown. I'm glad you feel that way. I want you here. I've missed you."

"Gram, I have something else to tell you. My wallet was stolen. And all my money that was in it. Moe paid me, you know, but it was all stolen and I didn't have the five dollars to give you that I'd promised. I was afraid to tell you."

"Gregory. Pay attention to me. You need never—*never*—be afraid to tell me anything. Except a lie. That I couldn't stand. I've got to know I can believe you. I've got to know that. Will you remember?"

"Yes. All right."

"From now on you can tell me anything at all. And don't worry about the five dollars. It isn't important. Anyway, we'll talk about that later." I paused as another remembrance struck me. How was I going to explain about the door lock?

"Gregory, there's one more thing we have to get straight. I had the doorlock changed, so you can't get in to my apartment anymore with the key you have."

"Gram! Why did you do *that?*"

"Well, when you didn't come home I got to thinking how all your friends—everybody at Artie's where you were living—knew you were staying with your grandmother and she was an old woman. I was sure they knew you had a key to my place, and I thought if you ever dropped it or lost it or anyone got it away from you—why, anybody, whether they knew me or not, could get in here and maybe—frighten me, Greg. I just didn't feel safe."

He was silent for a minute, then he said slowly, "Gram, I'm glad you did that. I think it was a wise thing for you to do."

"So now you understand that your key is no good. And I haven't any extra one for you"—I had given it to Fern—"so I'm going to have to let you in myself when you come. You'll have to ring my bell."

"Yes. Okay. And now will you come for me in a little while?"

"I'll be there in ten minutes, darling. I can take you over but I can't wait to bring you back. I'm doing a little baby-sitting this afternoon. You'll have to get yourself home."

"That's all right. I don't want you to wait. Sometimes it takes hours before the doctor comes. I'll hitchhike. I don't think I'll be very late."

I hung up, dazed, exultant. Then, sitting there by my phone, I put my hands to my face and felt tears running down. How thankful I was! How *deeply* thankful! *Praise the Lord,* I whispered softly to myself, over and over. *Praise the Lord! Oh, praise Him!*

"Nobody's ever going to change me." That was what Gregory had said. But he was on the way to changing himself. It was what we had been waiting for, hoping for—and it had happened. Suddenly the road ahead looked clear and easy.

Or was it? For I then realized that Gregory hadn't spoken of Ellen. *He* wanted to come to me. But did she? I still didn't know that answer.

I had a busy afternoon. I drove Gregory to Milltown and on the way we got everything explained and understood—except about Ellen. He didn't mention her and I felt he should bring up her name before I did. I couldn't understand his silence. Or—was the matter settled and I was supposed to know? Well, anyway, between Gregory and me there was trust again—and peace. We were both happy when I left him.

I went for Gregory's clothes at Fern's but she was not there so I found them where she had stacked them in a corner of the kitchen and took them home with me. Then I did my two hours of baby-sitting. Gregory had said he would be returning late, he thought, but anyway I knew better than to expect him for dinner. He would probably drift in around nine o'clock, I said to myself. With Ellen? Without Ellen? I wanted to know! But at nine he hadn't appeared. Nor at ten. At eleven—what was I to think? Should I worry? No. I was through with worry. I would trust Gregory. So I undressed and went to bed. I was tired but not a bit sleepy as I went over and over the events of the day. I knew I wouldn't sleep either until he came in, and I was sure I would hear the doorbell whenever he rang it.

The telephone rang instead. It was Gregory. He sounded—strange. Instantly I was alert. Ellen? Of course! He said, "Gram, I don't know what to do."

"What's the matter, Greg?"

"I'm at Artie's. And Ellen's not here. And it's midnight. So I don't know what to do. How much longer I should wait, I mean. What do you think?"

What could I think? He must have been planning to bring her—and she wasn't there to bring. But I had made it a rule never to decide anything for Gregory while he was with me. And never to give advice. Definitely I mustn't now. Ellen was *his* problem.

"Gregory, why don't you tell me the whole story?"

Well, he said, Ellen had taken Artie's car that afternoon while he, Gregory, was in Milltown. She had gone in it to get her unemployment check. But she hadn't come back and nobody in the house knew where she was. She hadn't telephoned or left any message about what she would do or where she would go after leaving the unemployment office, so he had waited expecting some kind of word. None had come and now it was midnight—and how much longer ought he to wait? "I thought she'd be here. I thought she wanted to come live with you, too. But now I don't know."

I asked him if he was married to Ellen? No! Of course not! He'd *told* me! "Well, then," I said, "be reasonable. If you aren't married she's not your legal responsibility, is she?" Reluctantly he agreed with me. "She's gone," I said. "She's gone off without telling you where, and you've waited more than a fair length of time for her to get in touch with you and she hasn't done that. Right? So it seems to me you can do what you *want* to do. What *do* you want to do, Gregory?"

"I want to come home to you, Gram. I want to get to bed so I can go to my job tomorrow at the church. I've got to! Moe's been so good to me, I've got to get there!"

"All right. Come, then. If that's what you surely want. Would you like me to pick you up at the monument? You won't be able to get a hitch at this hour of the night."

"Will you?"

"I'll be there in about five minutes."

Quickly I found my shoes and stockings, pulled on a dress over my nightgown, pulled a coat over that, and went out into the cold November night to drive two miles in order to pick up my nineteen-year-old grandson who was waiting for me. As I started my car I thought to myself that no one else I knew would do a thing like this. Everybody would call me a fool. But I had decided today that nothing was going to be too much for me from now on if I could at all help Gregory keep on the path he had chosen. I had embarked on this project and I was going to see it through to the end—which was not yet. I would stay with it—and him.

He was there in the shadows, moving about in nervous restlessness. Did I mind driving back past Artie's, he asked, to see if Ellen had returned after he had left. "You'll be safe, Gram. I'm with you and people know me and I have my knife. If she's there we'll see Artie's car that she's left in the empty lot next to his house. Here! Turn down this little alley. It's narrow but you can get through."

So I was finally to know where Artie lived.

Down the dark narrow alley I went, slowing when Gregory told me to and going on when he said, "It's not there. So she's not. We'd better go home."

I felt a stab of compunction. Not for Ellen but for him. I said, "Greg, you're really worried. Do you want to notify the police?"

He was horrified at the idea. That would be the very worst thing to do. I asked why. Because she was driving Artie's car, which wasn't registered. Gregory didn't know if it was a stolen car or not. But anyway, Artie had no registration for it, and if Ellen was picked up she'd be in a heap of trouble. "And she's in enough now," he finished. "You don't know what problems she has. We both have."

We went home, and as Gregory was too upset to think of sleeping we went to the kitchen and got something to eat and drink. I was glad he was so protective of his girl friend but I was annoyed with her and I could not help saying, "She wasn't very considerate of you, Greg, not letting you know anything about her or whether she was coming here with you."

"I know. I guess she still wasn't sure."

It was three o'clock before we finally turned out the lights, and even then I heard his TV long after that. I found it still on when I went to waken him in the morning to go to his job. We hadn't either of us slept much. But he pulled himself together and dressed promptly.

This was the day he was to appear at the clinic for his first dose of methadone. The clinic opened at ten o'clock and was open until noon. Gregory's arrangement with Moe was to get to the church at nine, put out the play equipment, leave with me at ten, get his dose, and return with me again as soon as possible to put the equipment back in the shed and to finish out a few more hours at work. Moe, who had a son of his own, as well as a Christian heart, was cooperative then and remained so about this loose schedule, as indeed the church did too.

That day when I went to pick him up, he told me that Ellen had telephoned him at church that morning. She had gone *home* last night! She had gone home because she was going to get off drugs too, and she wanted to start her treatments when Gregory did. But she was not eighteen yet so her mother had to sign her in. This she had to explain to her mother, who would drive her to the clinic this morning in order to do just that. Her mother would follow behind Artie's car which Ellen had borrowed. Then she would go back home again, and Ellen would take Gregory back to Edgewood with her in Artie's car.

"So you mustn't wait for me today, Gram. Moe understands. I told him I couldn't make it back today because Ellen will be having interviews and tests as I did, and it'll take her hours and she wants me with her. Of course, if you'd let me drive your car, Gram, I wouldn't have to bother you now or any time to go over there to the clinic."

But I was adamant about that, as I had been from the beginning. Gregory had been in too many accidents. He was too reckless. Too careless. I had established that until Ellen's car was fixed, I would take him wherever he wanted to go. So I just shook my head and he never brought up the subject again.

"I'm glad to hear Ellen is going off drugs too, Gregory. That's good news. You didn't tell me last night. Why didn't you?"

"I forgot it. It was settled, and I thought everything else was, too. About her coming to you with me, I mean. But then— well, you know what happened. I couldn't think, I was so mixed up about her." He drew a breath of relief. "Well, now she'll be free—signing up today —to start her doses only a day after me. Gram, I don't know how long it will take her to get through the preliminaries this afternoon, but we'll get back as early as we can."

We. There it was at last.

It was about six o'clock that afternoon when they finally came in together. I had decided to be as casual with Ellen as I had been with Gregory, so I greeted her without surprise.

"Ellen, I'm glad to see you. Gregory has told me you are going to stay here too."

She gave me a quick sidelong look. "Where will I sleep?"

"I told Gregory you could have the other bed in my room."

She was silent a moment. Then— "People are going to think we're here because we're married. What will you say?"

"If anyone asks I shall tell them you are not, but that I have room for you both and I'm glad to have you here."

She was silent again. And then, her face showing no emotion of any kind, she held up a paper bag she had been carrying and announced, "I brought some clothes with me. Where shall I put them?"

"This is Gregory's closet right here, Ellen. I think you'll find room there for your things, too." I gave her a smile and went quickly on. "Would you two like some dinner now? I have some frozen foods and it won't take long to fix something."

No. They didn't want any dinner. They had eaten late that afternoon in Milltown when they had finished at the clinic. They were going out again right away. They had some business to attend to. They would see me later.

I didn't ask what "later" meant. Or what the business was. Gregory had told me they had "problems." I hoped they would get them worked out soon.

It was after eleven o'clock that same night when the telephone rang. Gregory, I thought. But it was my daughter.

"Gregory wanted me to call you to tell you he didn't know when he and Ellen would get there. Does that mean she's with you, too?"

"Yes, Fern, it does."

"Mother!" She hadn't really expected that answer and I knew I had once again appalled my daughter. "I *told* you she'd be on your neck! How in the world—"

I broke in. "Fern, I haven't had a chance to tell you about this because you were still at the church when I stopped in to pick up Gregory's clothes. Actually, though, I wasn't sure then. Not until late today."

I heard Fern's exasperated groan. What a trouble I was to her, I thought, in a sorry mixture of impatience and amusement. What a worry! But I waited until she had let it all out with her usual explosiveness. "You must *really* be *completely* crazy. How are you going to manage? Are you going to let them *sleep* together? *We* never would! When she stayed here we sent her to the third floor. That's why they

went to Artie's! They had a room together down there. I *know* it! And now you— *Are* you? Is that what you're going to do? Let them?"

I broke in again. "Fern, listen. I've told Ellen she's to share my room with me." At this I heard a stunned silence. I hurried on. "Please don't say a word. Just keep still. Keep perfectly still. Let me remind you that this is *my* business. *My* project. *My* undertaking. And I'm going to work it out my own way."

"Now I *know* you're crazy. Oh, all right! Never mind! You're doing this! So I'll keep my mouth shut—if I can. I just called you to say they've been here. They came to borrow a tow rope. Gregory said they are going to get Ellen's car and tow it somewhere. He didn't say where. He just wanted me to let you know they'd be late getting to you but you are not to worry. They'll get there sometime around midnight." She hung up her receiver with a clatter.

It was later than midnight. It was after one o'clock when I heard a car pull quietly into our driveway, the low murmur of voices, the slam of a car door, and then the sound of someone pulling away. A moment later my bell rang and I opened to let Gregory and Ellen come in. They were wearing a weary look, yet they bore themselves with a jaunty air of jubilant triumph.

"We've just stolen Ellen's car," Gregory announced.

"You've *what?* What on earth do you mean?"

"It was Ellen's. It *is* Ellen's. But Artie's friend who's been working on it wouldn't let her have it. So we stole it."

It seemed that this friend of Artie's had finished doing the body work, which had been a good job for which Ellen had paid the amount agreed upon. But he had not been able to fix the motor. He could not get it to run. He wanted more money to work on it further—but Ellen wasn't willing to pay more.

"Ellen thinks he doesn't know enough about engines. And Artie thinks so too. But he wouldn't give her back her keys, so we decided we'd get the car away from him anyhow. I suppose you can call it stealing—or can you? It's really hers! Anyway, it was in an empty lot. Not in his or any garage. So it was no problem. The only problem was to take it when we were sure he wouldn't be around to catch us."

"I see."

"And we had to do it this late so the cops wouldn't catch Artie towing it. His car isn't registered, I told you. Remember?"

"Yes. I remember."

They stretched and laughed and threw their arms around each other in congratulatory joy. They had done it! They had outwitted the man who had been trying to outwit them! They had their car again! All they had to do now was get the motor fixed.

"Where did Artie leave it?" I asked.

"Where? Why here! It's right next to your car, Gram. You can see it in the morning."

They wanted to celebrate. There was more than the recovery of the car to celebrate. There was also their decision to give up drugs. We were all happy, so I joined them in the kitchen for Pepsi and cake. But presently I rose.

"I'm going to bed, darlings. Ellen, you may come into my room whenever you want to. I'll close my door now but I'll leave a night light on for you. It won't disturb me."

Ellen looked at me uncertainly. "You sure? I mean—Greg and I like to watch 'The Late Late Show.' We usually do—" She stopped, still uncertain, and threw a look at Gregory. He came to her rescue.

"Gram, I *never* turn the TV off till two o'clock. You know that!"

"Yes. I know. I understand. And you're good about keeping it turned down low. I'm sure I won't hear a thing. Goodnight."

They're here. They're both here. Thank You, God! It's going to work out. Oh, thank You!"

8

To every thing there is a season, and a time to every purpose under the heaven . . . A time to weep, and a time to laugh. . . .

Ecclesiastes 3:1, 4

The next day being Saturday, Gregory did not have to work at the church. But the clinic was open every day including holidays and Gregory had started receiving his methadone twice a day, morning and night. I must take him there both times for the next nine days, when he would be free, supposedly, of all desire for drugs. Ellen, however, had been accepted later than he and was not to begin her dosage until Monday, so she could sleep that morning. She was asleep when I got up, so Gregory and I went without her and reached the clinic promptly at ten o'clock.

The first thing he had to do upon arrival was wait his turn at the toilet in order to give a urine specimen for examination before he was permitted his own allowed amount of methadone. He took one quick look at the length of the line ahead of him near the water cooler and then turned to me.

"I'm not going to wait. It'll take too long."

I looked at him in surprise. How could he do without it, I wondered. But I did not want to ask. This was no time for me to hassle. He saw the question in my face, however, and volunteered a partial explanation. "I have plans," he said. So we went out to my parked car and back to my apartment. When Ellen, dressed except for putting on her shoes, heard what had happened, she said, "Greg! You should have waited! Now what will you do?"

I did not hear his reply, for I had already gone to my room and closed the door. But I could hear their voices getting more and more angry in some argument, and suddenly came a shout, quick stamping footsteps, and the shattering slam of my outside door. Gregory had flung out.

Ellen, standing in her stocking feet, faced me as I emerged from my room, a wild look on her face.

"He's gone."

"Where?"

"I don't know! He'll never come back! I can't do anything with him when he acts like this! He'll *never* come back! Oh, I've got to catch him!"

And then she, too, still in her stocking feet, ran out of the front door. It slammed again, but through it I could hear her wailing voice as she raced across the driveway calling Gregory's name. What would my neighbors be thinking?

Before I could answer myself she came dragging back, her face a mask of despair. "He wouldn't listen. He wouldn't stop. He's gone. And he'll never come back. Never! He wanted me to give him some money so he could go buy a methadone tablet from Artie, and I wouldn't do it. He said he had to have it if he was to last till tonight. But it was his fault because he wouldn't wait over there, so I wouldn't give it to him. And now he'll take heroin."

Would he? I didn't know. I knew so little about this drug business. Ellen knew better than I, I felt sure, but there was nothing either of us could do. In my mind everything—all hopes, all plans—had come to a crashing end if Ellen was right. I'd gone through a crashing end once! Must I again? I tried not to believe so and said, "He'll come back."

He did. Within half an hour. After I had made the beds and had sat down with a silent, despairing Ellen, there came a knock at the door and Ellen flew to open it. He came in looking shamefaced and guilty.

"I'm sorry, Ellen," he said.

She rushed into his arms. "I'll give you the money!" she cried. "I'll give it to you! Only don't leave me! Don't ever leave me!"

They were completely unmindful of me as they clung together. It was a poignant moment and I felt sympathy for them, but I also felt anger. However, I held my voice to quietness.

"Gregory and Ellen," I said. "Listen to me, both of you, for a moment. There can never again be such a scene as the one we've all just been through while you are staying with me. Never. Do you understand? You are not living in an isolated house separated from your neighbors by a wide lawn and big trees. There's only a wall between us and the people next door. And they, like all the others at this end of this apartment complex, are elderly. Most of them are widows living alone. Many of them are unwell. All of them are timid and mistrustful of young people. If you ever again go yelling out of my apartment they will complain of you, and you will be asked to leave. Perhaps I will be too. But this is my home and I want to stay. Well, now it's your home too, so if you also want to stay, you must promise me never to act like that again. Am I clear?"

They drew apart and looked at me in astonishment.

"I mean what am saying," I said, still quietly. "Decide now. Do you want to stay?"

There was a short silence; then Gregory said, "Yes, Gram. Of course we do." Ellen said nothing. I nodded at them both and left them to return to my room. A bit later Gregory went out, shutting the door softly behind him. He was gone for over an hour. When he returned he had a methadone tablet, which he showed me and which he divided with Ellen.

"The dose they give me at the clinic isn't strong enough, Gram. They don't believe I need any more. But I do. I know what I'm used to. I've got to have some extra. It's better for me to get methadone than go back to heroin. Ellen thinks so, too. So now I have this and I'll be careful of it. I won't take more than I need. Just a quarter of a tab. That leaves half that I'll save till tomorrow. *You* save it, Gram. *You* keep it for me. And only give it to me when I ask for it."

I took the tablet. I was getting much more involved in their lives than I wished to be. But before the day was over I was still more involved.

A little later they had what they called lunch. Gregory ate a big bowl of chocolate pudding, and Ellen made herself a ham sandwich. I had asked them if they had made any arrangements to get Ellen's car to the Volkswagen garage where they had said they were going to get it fixed, and they had replied that they had telephoned to find out how late it would be open on Saturday.

"They don't close till six," Gregory reported to me.

"Is Artie going to tow it there for you?"

"He can't, Gram! He wouldn't dare to do that in the daylight!"

It was then I made my offer. Why not? Hadn't I towed Gregory's car—the first one he had ever had—from the yard where he had bought it to his house only a few years ago? There had been no trouble then. Why should there be now? It seemed the simplest thing to do. The obvious thing. They were anxious to get that car in shape and I was anxious to have them. It would relieve me of all their trips to the clinic. Besides, it was taking up space in the driveway that properly belonged to tenants here. Gregory would not have asked this of me. He had been planning to ask some boy he knew to help him. But when I offered he accepted with gratitude and surprise and thanked me warmly. Was I sure I wanted to do this? Was I sure I could do it? Well, thanks again. Then he and Ellen fell asleep on the sofa bed after their lunch.

I woke them a little after three. Already the winter sun was slanting toward the west. I wanted to get this job done before dark. They pulled themselves together and we all put on our warm coats and went out to inspect the tow rope. It was a sorry-looking object. Badly frayed and worn, and knotted in two or three places where it had been broken.

"Do you think it will hold?" I asked Gregory.

"It's all we have, Gram. Do you want to try it?"

"Well, I think if we go slowly enough and have luck at the lights so I don't have to stop and start again—"

We set out. It was only two miles on a straight and level road and there were only three lights to worry about. We had good fortune on the first two, but the third, at a main intersection, was red. We stopped. Gregory, sitting beside me, fidgeted.

"Start up real slow, Gram," he said. "Ellen's scared to death. Can you see her face in your mirror?" Ellen was at the wheel of her car.

I started slowly, but in spite of my care, the rope pulled apart. Instantly Gregory was out of my car, speaking urgently to me through the window.

"Keep on, Gram! Keep going! I'll push Ellen across! We can't hold up traffic or a cop will come. Keep on! And park at the curb there on the opposite corner!"

I did as he said. The next moment we were lined up, Ellen behind me, across the street, and Gregory was examining the frayed old rope. It was useless, and the air was blue with the four-letter words Gregory used.

"It's just no good, Gram! There's no use trying. It's no good. It's *gone.*"

I looked about. There was a variety store just down the block that I knew carried about everything. I gave Gregory some money and told him to go buy some rope.

"We're almost there, Greg. We've got to make it. We can't leave your car here all night."

"I know. Okay."

Ellen went with him. I was left on guard over the two cars beneath a sign that distinctly said NO PARKING. I stood there, shivering in the wintry air, seeing the dusk gather and hoping no policeman would appear to question me.

In a few moments they reappeared, jubilant, with a length of nylon rope in Gregory's hands.

"This should do it," he said, and he got busy fastening the two cars together. In a moment Ellen was in hers again and he was beside me in mine.

"Take it easy now, Gram," he said.

I nodded. But—stupidly—I forgot to release my brakes, and at the first tug the new rope broke as if it were made of straw. Gregory— furious—was out again to inspect the damage in an instant. Yes, he could tie it once more, he said, but the rope was much shorter now; the cars would be only about five feet apart. He was tense as he pulled out his knife from his belt and sliced off the frayed part in order to knot together what was left. When he returned to me he was the captain in command of a perilous situation.

"Listen, Gram. Are your brakes off now? Are you sure? Yes? Then all right. Listen! At the very next corner there's a light. We have to turn left there. Whether that light is red or green, *turn left there.* Then there's only one short block *up hill* to the next corner, where there's another light. *Never mind!* Go *through* it! I'll be with you—and if the light is red, I'll jump out and stop the traffic so you can get across. The Volkswagen place is directly across that street. It's directly oppo- site—and you go right into it. You've *got* to get there, Gram! It's almost six o'clock. You're *got* to make it! Understand? After you turn left at the next corner *don't stop for anything!* Not a red light or *anything!* Are you ready? Okay! *Go!*"

I nodded. Slowly, carefully, I let in my clutch. Slowly, carefully I inched forward. Ellen was rolling smoothly along behind me. The rope was holding. We were all right.

At the corner the light was red. "Turn just the same, Gram! Like I said! Turn left here and *keep going!* It's up hill now and that's too bad, but you've got to make it. If you stop, we're *stuck!* We'll never dare start up on the hill. We'll roll back down and that'll be the *end.* So—*don't stop for anything!*"

I nodded, my eyes on the light ahead. It was green up there. Could I reach it before it changed? I didn't dare speed up at all. I didn't dare risk a stronger pull. We were doing all right! We really were. In my little mirror I could see Ellen's face. It was stiff with fear as she gripped her wheel.

We were nearly there when the light turned yellow. Gregory sprang out as if he had been shot. He was shouting at me.

"Never mind! Keep going, Gram!. I'll stop the traffic!"

He did. I saw the light turning inexorably red. I saw his long lean figure as he leaped out into the maelstrom of traffic. I was aware of his arms flailing wildly, signaling to me to come on and to the drivers all around him to stop. Faintly I heard the squeal of brakes, the honking of horns, angry voices. Dimly I saw furious faces, startled faces. But the cars did indeed halt before that intrepid figure; there was an open space for me, and I went sailing through it, Ellen trailing safely behind.

It wasn't until instructions had been given to the mechanic who took over Ellen's car, and when we were all squeezed into the front seat of my old Chevy again on the way back to my apartment, that Gregory said, "Did you forget, Gram?"

"Forget what?"

"That it's against the law in Edgewood for any but a tow truck to tow."

"Gregory! Forget! I never even *knew* it! Why didn't you tell me?"

"I thought you knew. I thought everybody knew."

But that night as I slipped between the sheets of my bed before Ellen joined me, I suddenly began laughing softly to myself. For I had a picture of me at the wheel of my car, a solid, stolid figure, driving with all the stateliness and dignity in the world and blissfully unmindful of rules and regulations, right through the miraculously opened avenue that had been made in the chaos around me to get my grandson's sweetheart's car to its destination.

"Gram," I said aloud to myself, "for a women in her eightieth year, you are living a very strange life."

It was to become still stranger.

9

Call unto me, and I will answer thee, and shew thee great and mighty things, which thou knowest not.

Jeremiah 33:3

It was the Monday after the car-towing incident and I was taking Gregory to the clinic for his morning dose. Ellen was not with us. She had gone again to her distant home on Sunday. Some friend of hers —a girl she knew—had taken her there. She had had to break the news to her mother that her car was still not fixed and would require more money than she herself could afford. Her mother was somehow to explain this to her father, who was still in the dark about there having been an accident at all. Ellen did indeed have troubles, as Gregory had said, and I was glad I was not responsible for straightening them out. Her mother was to bring her to the clinic, and Gregory would meet her there, and they would both return with me.

That was the plan anyway. But it did not work out that way at all. For that morning at the church, before I went for him, Gregory had not been able to wait to reach the clinic and had relieved himself. So, unable so soon again to offer the required specimen, he stood by the water cooler, drinking cup after cup as he tried to hurry himself along and getting madder by the minute. Ellen had not yet arrived.

"This isn't going to do any good," he fumed to one of the staff who had come out into the hall from his office at that moment. "It never does! I could drink water all day and it wouldn't help. Nothing helps but wine. If I had wine—"

"Well, there's no wine here and you shouldn't drink it in any case."

"I've drunk wine! I've drunk plenty of wine! It never hurt me!"

To be told what he should or should not do was adding fuel to the fire. I saw Gregory's eyes flashing as he got ready for an argument.

I heard his voice getting louder and louder.

"You people!" he stormed. "You think you're helping us! But you aren't! Not really. You have all these rules and regulations! You ought to let me have—"

I stepped close to him and touched him on the arm.

"Gregory. Let's go take a little walk." And I laid my hand on his arm.

To my surprise he subsided and came with me down the hall and out the front door. It was a cold raw rainy day. I had been suffering with arthritis for a long time and ignoring it. But my left leg ached its whole length continually so I had to walk with a limp. I wanted to use a cane but out of consideration for Gregory I didn't. It seemed to me that it was embarrassing enough for him to have his grandmother carting him back and forth twice a day in her car, but if I appeared on a cane it would be too much. So I always took care to walk behind him. Then he could, with impunity, act as if I were not associated with him. Or at least he wouldn't be so conscious of his old nursemaid-grandmother.

But today I simply had to hold on to his arm. At the porch steps I looked out at the slanting curtain of rain and the big puddles in the square before us, and I asked him if he knew where there was a liquor store. He did. It was only three or four blocks away.

"Let's go," I said. "But I'll have to lean on you."

Down the steps we went. I knew why he hadn't said this time, as he had before, that he wouldn't wait because he had "other plans." It was for the reason that he had no plans. He knew very well that Ellen had no money left to buy him any methadone tablets, and that they both had to subsist on what was given them at the clinic until her next check came.

And I knew this because of what had happened Sunday night when, on returning from the clinic, I had dropped them off in Edgewood at Artie's. They had said that they might be late getting home but I was not to worry. Artie was taking them in to New York to celebrate the recovery of Ellen's car. He had had a hand in that and he wanted a party. "Don't worry," they had repeated to me.

I didn't. I was tired out and I went to bed early. My doorbell had rung several times before I was awake enough to realize that Gregory and Ellen were waiting to get in. I turned on my light, put on my dressing gown, and looked at the clock. It was exactly three in the morning. I padded to the door and opened it for them. They came in looking both radiant and guilty—and stood waiting for my words. They themselves said nothing either in apology or explanation. I said nothing either.

For I could read on their faces what they were thinking: Yes, it's terribly late. But so what? We're free, independent adults. We don't have to tell you where we've been or what we've been doing. We don't have to make any report or any excuses. That isn't in the contract if we live here. What we do is our business.

This was what they were defiantly thinking, at the same time fully expecting an angry blast from me, as it might have been deserved and given elsewhere. But all I said was, "Hi. I'm glad you're back. If you're hungry, help yourselves to whatever you want. I'm going back to bed."

At that they both broke into speech simultaneously. They had gone to New York, as they'd said. In Artie's car. They had gone to a movie and then someplace to eat. They'd heard three different bands. One had seven pieces. It was great.

"I'm glad you had such a good time. But I'm still going to bed. Goodnight, my dears. Or is it morning?"

And that was exactly why Gregory had now to wait at the clinic to get his dose. They had spent all their money in riotous, glorious living in celebration of having got their car successfully to a good garage.

Plodding along now beside him, I thought that Gregory's anger had revealed how very much he wanted to stay on this program, and I wasn't going to let him miss his chance if all he needed was some wine. I was sure too that he knew himself better than anyone else and that the remonstrance of the staff member about wine had been an automatic response because there were other boys standing around listening to what he might say.

We reached the liquor store. He bought the wine of his choice. We plodded back. I told him we would have to sit in the car while he drank what he needed, for if he was seen with a bottle he would be in trouble. He agreed and we sat there. Gregory drank fitfully and we talked in a desultory fashion. Presently I limped into the house to see if Ellen was there yet and to tell her where we were. But she had not come.

Suddenly Gregory exploded again. Hell! This was no good! He was only getting drunk! He wasn't any nearer being ready for the toilet than he had been an hour ago! That was the trouble with a setup like this! It never really helped you! He hadn't been given enough methadone since he'd started there. And each day as the amount was reduced he was getting less and less! Well, he wasn't going to go on with this rigamarole! He was *through.* He was through with the whole nonsensical business, which wasn't going to work anyway! So I could take him home. Ellen's mother could bring her when Ellen found he wasn't there. He jammed the cork in the neck of the bottle, shoved it down into his coat pocket, and finished in a low, furious voice, "Start your car, Gram! I tell you I'm *through!"*

I had no choice. Gregory was in such a mood he was impossible to reason with or even talk to. Fern had warned me. Now I was experiencing it. But I was absolutely sick at heart to think that again, just at the beginning of this hopeful reform—perhaps the start of a new life for him—he was ending it.

Without a word I turned on the ignition, started my car, and we headed out of the driveway toward home. This battle to get off drugs was anything but an easy one, as Gregory's counselor had told me. I had had a few talks with her while waiting around for Gregory and I knew her to be a sympathetic woman, competent and wise.

"They fight us," she had said. "Gregory's not the only one who thinks our doses aren't strong enough. They all say that. But it's only a mental block with them. The doses really are sufficient to set them free. They just don't want to believe it. They don't want to lose their dependence on something. They're really afraid. That's a large part of it. They're afraid to let go. So don't accept all Gregory tells you. He'll make the grade. I've talked with him. I've watched him. I've taken a real interest in him and I'm sure he'll make the grade. He has a very strong character. He's made of good stuff. And his background is better than that of most of the boys and girls here. He'll make it! Just don't let him use you. Don't let him get away with anything. And never, never give him any money to go buy something off the streets."

These things she had said to me and I was remembering them now. How right was she? Was some improvement possible in their program? I didn't know.

I didn't know anything except that there was nothing I could do or say to this boy beside me, sunk now in a bitter silence. I was silent too, driving slowly for the rain was still coming down and making the streets slippery with a slight glaze of ice in places. Besides, I kept hoping that at some moment Gregory would change his mind and ask me to turn around and take him back. I kept waiting for that word.

But it didn't come. On we went, getting nearer and nearer to home and nearer and nearer to his total defeat. Because if he once dropped out, the rule was that he would not be given a second chance. I was at the corner where we were to turn left to cross the tracks, with the apartment complex just a short block beyond and in plain sight, when he spoke in a low voice.

"You know, Gram. I think I could go now. I think I could, really."

"You do, Greg? You do, truly? Well, then, let's *go!*"

And I swung the wheel to the right instead of to the left and raced up the road that would lead us back to the clinic, eight miles and half an hour away.

"Never mind, Gram, don't bother," I heard him say.

But his protest was feeble and I knew by its weakness, as I had known by his anger earlier, that he wanted to stay on that program more than he wanted anything else. It had been his choice. His own decision. Just now he had acted impulsively and he regretted it. But it was not too late, and my voice sang as I answered him.

"It's okay, Gregory! We've got time before the clinic closes. We'll make it! Oh, darling, I'm so *glad!*"

The ride back was almost as silent as the ride home had been. I had to go faster than I liked, for we hadn't many minutes to spare—and we had to get there. We simply had to! With luck we could do it. With luck—

We had the luck. We were within a few blocks of the building and I drew a breath of relief.

"Gregory! We hit *no* red lights! Do you realize that? The Lord is with us!"

He made no answer. For no reason I had a memory of Gregory's first experience in Tennessee when he had explored various churches, different isms, finding them interesting. And I wondered if he ever thought about such things now. So I put a question to him.

"Gregory, do you believe in God these days?"

"He's never done anything for me," was his somewhat surly reply. And then he began to tell me of the time just last week when Ellen had taken an overdose of heroin. "That was really the reason why she decided to give up drugs," he said. "She'd been scared. She was out cold. Her nails were turning blue. I thought she was really gone. But I used mouth-to-mouth resuscitation on her. I knew how to do it. So I worked on her and brought her back. And when she came to, she began laughing and crying and saying, 'Oh, thank God! I'm still alive! I'm still here! Thank God!' And it made me mad. So I asked her why she was thanking God when it was me who'd saved her. It was me she ought to thank, I told her. Not God."

We were turning into the clinic driveway. I spoke quickly.

"I suppose, Gregory, that it could have gone the other way. Couldn't it? You might not have saved her, I mean. Right?"

"Well—maybe. I suppose so—"

"So how do you know, darling, that God didn't give you the power to save her? Did you ever think of that?"

"No."

"Well, give it a thought, Greg. Give it a thought. He was with us just now, I'm sure." (And I had called it *luck,* I remembered.)

That night I wrote in my diary—"I think I did the right thing with Greg today. And I do truly believe everything will work out now. To success." I read this over. It seemed arrogant. It *was* arrogant. Prideful! I added three words: "Thank You, God."

10

A man that hath friends must shew himself friendly. . . .

Proverbs 18:24

Success, I was to learn, meant many things. Sometimes it meant only a narrow escape from disaster—as yesterday had been. Sometimes it meant complications that must be ironed out before the road to success could be followed again.

Such a time was the day soon after when Gregory, borrowing Artie's car, was stopped by police on his way home. Having no registration card to show, he was arrested on the charge of "fictitious plates" and the car was impounded.

I happened to be at my daughter's when he telephoned there, having first tried to reach me at the apartment with no results. And it was I who answered the ring of the telephone.

"Gram? Gram, I'm in jail."

"Gregory! Whatever *for?*"

"I got caught driving Artie's car. I've been driving it for weeks and never got caught before. But now I need fifty dollars to get out of here. Can you help me?"

He sounded so unperturbed! What was fifty dollars? It was a good deal to me and I told him I didn't have it.

"Is Dad there?"

It was a Sunday so he was, and I called him. He came to the phone immediately and when he heard the story he shook his head. But he said, "All right, Greg. I'll be there in a few minutes."

I thought— After all he's spent on that boy! Private schools, psychiatrists, lawyers. I said, "You're good, Tom."

He shrugged. "So are you. And I think he, too, is really trying to be now. So—" He shrugged again.

"Did he ever help you with your storm windows?"

"No."

I was bothered by that, as well as by Tom's continuing generosity. Gregory took and took, I told myself. And what did he give back but trouble? He had known the risk involved in driving Artie's car. Would he never stop taking chances? If he ever thought at all of what he owed his father, it didn't seem to worry him. He owed Ellen money too. And her friend, Betsy, who let them use her car occasionally and who had had to have repair work done on it after Gregory had driven it once too fast, too far without oil. That bill was hanging over him right now, too.

Clearly, the road to success (and what exactly did I mean by that?) was not going to be smooth and easy. Would he never learn? I had to trust to time. I had to *trust*. That was the thing. I had to trust.

But there were high moments as well as low ones, I discovered.

There was the day following Tom's rescue of him when Gregory unexpectedly took me into his confidence. Ellen, gone to Betsy's, was not there. He said he wanted to show me something and he went to his closet and brought out a pair of his heavy sox, rolled up into a ball. From this he took out a syringe, a needle, and a bent silver teaspoon.

"The spoon is the cooker," he explained. "You put the powder in it and light a match under it and it melts right away. Then with the syringe you're set for a fix. I could be fined fifty dollars if I was caught with this."

"Why do you keep it then, Gregory? Now that you're on methadone."

"I don't know. I might need it some time. But I may sell it for five dollars if I can find a buyer for it. I have contacts. I'll think about it."

He put it away again, but after he had left me I wondered. Why had he shown it to me, anyway? Was he just boasting of what he dared possess? Or did he want to get rid of it, couldn't quite make up his mind and—obliquely—was asking for help? I had no way of knowing.

But when, a bit later, I found myself alone with Ellen, I decided to tell her of the incident. She had been with me only a day or so but already I knew her to be a much more practical person than Gregory. She knew far better than he the value of money and handled hers with care. She acted on reason, too, rather than on impulse. Furthermore,

I felt that if I could win her confidence, as I had Gregory's, she might be able to help me in this battle against drugs, because she was not as dependent on them as he was. I had seen her clearheaded when he was not. This gave her an advantage over him. And if, at those times, I could enlist her on my side, it might be a good thing. So I spoke with sudden directness.

"Gregory showed me his syringe outfit today," I said.

She was patently surprised. How had he come to do that, she asked. I told her I didn't know. I told her he had said it was hers as much as his.

"It is." She then asked me what I was going to do with it. I thought for a minute, not sure yet whether her words meant she was with me or not. Then I said, "I'd rather let you handle this, Ellen, since it's yours too."

Her face revealed no reaction to my gesture. She said only, "Where is it? I can find a buyer all right."

I told her, she nodded, and later that same day when they had both gone out, I wondered if she would really do anything with it, or if she already had. That evening I heard them both talking. He was accusing her of taking the outfit.

"It's not there," I heard him say. "Nothing but the silver spoon is there. You must have taken it."

"Well, you owed me five dollars."

"I know. I was going to pay you. I have a good thing coming up. I'm going—" His voice died away and I heard no more. I speculated what the good thing might be, but I put away the question. I thought only that I was glad he hadn't been angry with Ellen. The next day when they were both gone, I found the little silver spoon and put it in my paper bag of trash which I carried to the cellar. When I saw him again I told him what I had done. "I knew Ellen had sold the syringe and needle, so why keep the spoon, Gregory?" I asked.

He smiled a bit ruefully. "It was sterling silver, Gram. I could have gotten some money for it."

"You need money? Is that what you meant when you said you had a good thing coming up? I heard you and I wondered."

"Well, Gram, we have to live, you know. We need things. And Ellen's got all she can take care of with her car."

They were dealing. I knew they were dealing. They bought drugs to sell. And marijuana. They always thought they would get ahead. I knew this and the knowledge troubled me, but nothing I could say would change their ways. They would just say, "We have to do it, Gram! We *have* to!"

It was about now that there came a change in Gregory. I had never, since he had come to me, heard any of that obscene language his parents had feared I would hear. He had always restrained himself—except on that memorable trip to the Volkswagen garage. But there had been nothing since then. Now he was extraordinarily polite, remembering his *please*s and *thank-you*s, opening doors to let me go through first, holding them open for me to enter. He volunteered to carry my trash basket to the cellar for me every morning too. He would say, "I'll make the bed, Gram." Or— "Would you like me to mop your kitchen floor for you?" Or— "I can weed your garden if you'd like me to." This return to basic sweetness and thoughtfulness was, I thought, most promising and significant. As I had hoped and expected, Gregory was different with me. He was calm. He acted pulled-together. Still irresponsible, still unreasoning sometimes, but definitely he was easier to live with than he'd been at Fern's.

If only he could get to sleep before two o'clock in the morning. If only he would stop taking the downers that he thought made sleep possible. If only he would believe that the methadone he was getting would work a cure on him, as he had been told it would— But he had a fixation on that subject. And it did not bear my thinking about. I concentrated on gratitude for the quiet and for the change that even his small doses seemed to have brought about in him. We were running on an even keel, I told myself, and both Ellen and Gregory were content to be with me. That would have to be enough.

I had yet to establish the order in our days that I had wanted and had hoped to have. Except for our trips to the clinic morning and night, there was no order. I never knew when they would come in, when they would want to eat—if at all—when they would go out. Night was turned into day and day into night. Gregory's sofa bed sometimes was not made up until the middle of the afternoon. Dishes used for a snatched meal were left dirty in the sink with the words "I'll do them later."

And then there were all of their friends.

At first I had told Gregory they could not come to my apartment. I remembered clearly how they had swarmed into Fern's kitchen— six or eight at a time—to smoke, leaving butts and ashes all over her table, her counter, her floor—to argue in loud voices—to use her telephone for endless hours while they planned their mysterious activities for that day or that night or tomorrow. It had been confusion compounded and I had thought— Enough is enough, and Ellen and Gregory were enough. So I had said, "Gregory, I would rather your friends didn't come here. Or even telephone you. Find some other meeting place and some other telephone, will you, please?"

He had turned and looked at me in shocked surprise. "But Gram! How can I do *that?* They're my *friends!* You mean they can't call me up at *all?* And I can't ask them here either? Why, Gram! They're boys just like me! Why *not?*"

Why not indeed? What was I trying to do anyway? I had offered Gregory a home. What kind of home would it be if his friends couldn't telephone him or come see him? I must be out of my mind. Quickly I changed my tune.

"Well, all right. But there'll have to be restrictions. I'm not sure exactly what you talk about—or feel you have to talk about—at such great length on the phone. But whatever it is, you can't do it here. I won't condone what I don't know. So you can't arrange for any deals —any underhanded business, anything like that, if that is what it is —on my line. Clear?" He nodded and I went on. "And when they come here to see you and Ellen, it's a *social* call entirely. Nothing else. You may eat, drink, smoke, and talk all you want. But there are to be *no* drug transactions—no getting or giving marijuana in my apartment." I looked at him and waited. He nodded again. I added—"And please use the ashtrays." He nodded a third time. And so it was settled, without hassling, and I knew a moment of deep satisfaction.

Did they come? I should say they did! I had decided to greet them when they first appeared and before I withdrew to my bedroom. This caused some hesitancy and uncertainty on their part at first. They felt my presence was an intrusion, probably entailing supervision and certainly condemnation. But this passed when they found instead that I was friendly and truly interested in listening to their talk. This was all of their jobs, their hopes, their plans for the future. There were no lewd jokes. Once I heard one boy say to a newcomer who was hanging back at the door, "Come on in! It's all right. She's not like other grandmothers." This immensely pleased me. And though, in the beginning, with their uniform beards, long hair and shirttails hanging out over identical blue jeans, they all appeared alike to me, I soon discovered that if I looked past all their hair directly into their eyes, each person was different, each was interesting, and each was likable for one reason or another. That was a surprise. I hadn't expected to like them.

There was Nick. He had an Afro haircut that surrounded a pair of alert friendly eyes. I concentrated on his eyes and we began talking. He spoke in a pleasantly modulated tone in fluent English. Was he a college lad, I asked. No, he wasn't. But maybe he would be some day. He didn't know. He was thinking about it because he liked books and reading but right now he was working in a real-estate office. Not selling land, of course. He wasn't qualified to do that. His job was to make the initial contacts from a long list taken from the telephone book and given him by the office. If he could interest a party sufficiently, then he made a date for one of the staff to follow up the lead.

I asked him if he found this work appealing. Not very, he told me, except that it paid well. Three dollars an hour and you could work as many hours a day as you chose. But it was the same thing over and over. The same line of talk, trying to sell yourself. He'd liked surfing better. Yes, he had been a surfer up and down the East Coast. It had been good sport. But he couldn't do it anymore. He wasn't fit. He was all out of condition.

"Because of drugs?"

He nodded. But he might get back to that fun some day. He hoped, anyway. He was on methadone now. His doctor gave it to him regularly. He shouldn't. It was illegal. But money was no problem in his family.

I asked him how he came to get on methadone. He looked straight at me as he answered. "I realized I was killing myself. It was as simple as that. So I asked myself if I wanted to live." He paused. "We all of us get to that point sooner or later, Mrs. Randall," he finished.

"And do you think Gregory is there now?" I asked.

"Yes. I think so. He's started the treatment. I think he's where I

was a few months ago. He's weighing it all up. I also think it's good
he's with you."

"Will you help him along if he ever needs help?"

"I sure will."

And I knew he would. I knew what a tightly knit and loyal group
they were. They helped each other with anything and everything.
With drugs, addresses, money—with whatever seemed to be needed
at the moment. One of the reasons Gregory was always in debt was
that when he had money he handed it over generously to anyone who
asked him for it.

It seemed to me that Ritchie's beard covered all of his face except
his nose. But above that I found eyes that were regarding me with a
quiet contemplation. I moved toward him and opened the conversation.

He had been in Vietnam. He hadn't been wounded, no. He'd been
lucky that way. But he was glad when his term of duty was ended and
he was home again. Now he was helping his father, who was a builder
of houses. Yes, he had brothers and sisters. Too many. The house was
hectic sometimes. That's why he had been glad to get away into the
service for a while. And since he'd come back things were not quite
so bad as they had been, because a couple of his sisters had got
married.

Still it was not exactly a restful place in which to live. It didn't suit
him anyway. And he would be glad when his father retired, as he was
going to do soon. Then he himself would be given his father's tools,
and what he was going to do was build a house for himself way out
in the country somewhere and live alone. When he got settled in it
he would start working for other people. Building houses. He knew
how. In time he would have his own business. No, he wouldn't be
lonely. He thought it was the best way to live. For him anyway. Yes,
he was on drugs. But not much. He could manage without them most
of the time. And he gave me a rather sweet and gentle smile.

He and Nick, the boy with the Afro haircut, and several others with
whom I talked—the one who made doorknobs for a hobby, the one
who was taking a course in computers in a night school, the one who
liked to draw cartoons—were all ahead of Gregory. They all had
regular jobs or clear objectives. To be sure, they dealt in drugs, chiefly

marijuana, on the side, but they considered that no crime. It was a way, they explained, to make extra money they needed. It was that simple, they said. And it was fun. It was an exciting thing to do—to outwit the Establishment—and as long as you didn't get caught, it was all right. They really believed that. They had no sense of guilt at all. They felt they were simply being rational in an irrational world.

And someday—someday they could see themselves living exactly as they pleased, with no need, no desire, to carry on this dangerous illicit business. They did not say it quite that clearly to me but I knew it was in their minds. I felt it and was encouraged for my grandson. Someday for him too, I thought—however long it might take him to get there. And however long *that* might be, I would stay by him.

Not as many girls came as boys did. Only two or three to the ten or more of their hairy accomplices. And the girls were far less trusting of me. They sat close together in a self-conscious silence, offering only monosyllables for replies and peering out from between their long veils of straight hair that draped the two sides of their faces. They smiled. They giggled. But they were patently waiting for some mysterious signal that would lift them all up to depart in a body.

One night when there must have been a dozen of these young persons milling about between my living room and the kitchen, I found myself standing behind my high wing chair next to the small table where lay Gregory's radio, cigarettes, ashtray, and his stout-handled, wicked-looking hunting knife that he always wore when he went out on some of his business deals.

My glance fell on it, then traveled around the room. Everyone was busily engaged and no attention was being paid to me. So— why not? Unnoticed, I stretched down a hand, picked up the knife, laid it along the inside of my arm and, still unnoticed, moved quietly toward my bedroom. Once inside there, I opened my closet door, reached up to a carton of Christmas decorations, and dropped that lethal weapon down into the bottom of the box. There it lay safely unseen until the next day, when I took it to the cellar and buried it in a trash barrel there.

Now, I thought with considerable contentment, the syringe and the needle and the knife were all gone.

I never heard Gregory say anything about its disappearance. I'm sure he believed one of his friends had taken it that night. But they *were* his friends, so how could he question them?

Thank You for this too, God.

Then there was the night when Gregory, who, with Ellen, had been watching "The Late Late Show" on TV until long after midnight, knocked on my door, having seen my light on under it.

"Gram?"

"Yes, darling?"

"Will it bother you if we go out in the kitchen and make some cupcakes now?"

"No. Have fun. Just be sure and clean up afterwards."

What did it matter? That was the pattern of their lives—if you could call it a pattern. That was the crazy way they ate. Sweets or nothing at all when they were on drugs. Milk and hamburgers when they weren't. Quarts and quarts of milk. I bought two gallon containers every day. And cupcakes at midnight.

Ups and downs. But more ups than downs during that period of our lives together. More hope. And no idea of the troubles and trials that lay ahead.

11

Now therefore thus saith the Lord of hosts; Consider your ways.
Ye have sown much, and bring in little. . . .

Haggai 1:5, 6.

I tried to carry on my own life as usual while those two young
people were with me. There was always the hasty tidying up of my
apartment and the daily shopping, but there were also meetings with
friends, business meetings of some kind, a luncheon or a tea where I
must be present, and occasional calls on people I knew who were ill
in nursing homes. It was a strain to do all this because of my rheuma-
tism and with my nights broken by sleeplessness as I waited for
Gregory's light to go out and for Ellen to join me, or for the two of
them to return from somewhere, and I was beginning to feel a great
weariness. But no matter how I felt I took him to his church work
in the morning and the two of them to the clinic for their doses of
methadone both night and morning.

I was glad that Thanksgiving was coming and Ellen was to go to
her home for the holiday. Her car was not yet fixed and her father was
insisting that she explain what had happened to it, why it was costing
so much, and why it was necessary for her to stay away from her
family during the repair work. He was not aware of the visits to the
clinic, for he had never been told she was on drugs and was now trying
to get off. Her mother knew—had had to know to arrange Ellen's
admission—and she wanted Ellen now to help her break the story to
her father. Thanksgiving would be a good time to do it, she had said.
There would be a family gathering, and the presence of others at the
table would offer diversion at those moments when questioning became difficult. Again I was glad I was not responsible for Ellen's
troubles. (She was to be gone overnight.)

Gregory and I were expected at Fern's house. There would be just the five of us, and I was hopeful of a pleasant day. Bruce had long ago accepted Gregory's living with me with gratitude and was resigned to Gregory's presence for the few hours we would be there. Fern herself would remember not to hassle Gregory in any way, as I was sure Tom would, too.

We arrived early and since there was time before dinner Gregory went up to his room to oil his high boots, which were his prize possession.

I went up with him while he worked, and as we entered I saw the storm windows he had never hung stacked up against one wall. I said nothing. Gregory turned on his big radio, which he had left there, and we listened to music until the news came on. Then Gregory, nearly through with his polishing, snapped it off.

I said casually, "Gregory, here are the windows you never hung for your father. How about doing them now? They need washing first, but I'll help you."

He said that was a good idea, so I went to the kitchen for a pail of water and some cloths. We worked together and when Fern called us to dinner the last window had been cleaned and hung in its place. I was pleased. It seemed to me that an advance had been made in a family relationship that had never really ended and that might be fully restored in time. I gave quiet thanks for this small success.

The dinner was delicious, the hour relaxing and peaceful. Gregory helped carry the plates out to the kitchen afterward and I sensed then that it was time for us to depart while everything was so good. Indeed it had been almost too good, not only that day, I thought, but for the last several days. The methadone, whatever he thought about it, had really worked wonders in establishing a calm all around. And weren't the doses proving sufficient, even though Gregory didn't think so and was still talking about getting on the maintenance program when his nine days were up?

He was quiet and gentle when we reached home, as indeed he had been the whole time we were at Fern's. And he was in an unusually communicative mood.

We sat side by side on the sofa and he began telling me how it happened that Ellen's car had been so badly smashed up. They had gone in to New York, to the Bronx, for drugs. It was not unusual for them to do this. Gregory said he was then having to get ninety dollars' worth of the heroin every day because his need was so great. "It just built up," he said. "I had to have it. So I was working round the clock, just about, to make that much money." (No wonder he had been exhausted all the time, I thought.) "The church money was only peanuts. And I couldn't let Ellen pay for everything. I hardly ever slept. I just *had* to have the stuff, that's all. Sometimes Ellen went with me. Sometimes I went alone. That time she was with me."

He knew where to go, he said. He had been there before. But the locals didn't like outsiders coming there to take what they themselves wanted. They had ganged up on him that time, and when he got back to the car where Ellen was waiting, he found it had been blocked by a big truck which had been parked slantwise in front of it and by another that had pulled up close behind. There was no way for them to get out and away.

"Then everybody began throwing things at us," he told me. "Sticks, stones, rocks, bottles—anything and everything. All we could do was sit there listening to all that stuff coming down on us and wonder if we'd ever get out of there alive. The windshield was hit but luckily didn't break. Just cracked all the way down. Ellen began crying. She was scared to death."

I sat listening to his words in a shocked silence as I glimpsed the life he had been living before he came to me. I had had no idea of the pressure that had been on him or the wildness of his days—or the danger, the dreadful danger, in which he had lived during his frenzied desire and search for drugs. I understood much better now everything Moe had said to me that day when Gregory had not appeared at church.

He went on.

Suddenly, he didn't know why, the truck in front of them pulled away. Maybe they thought the police were coming. He had no idea. But it was his chance, and he shot out of there at a clip of about ninety miles an hour. He had kept up that pace until he was safely back in Edgewood again, but when he reached Artie's he couldn't shut off the motor. It just kept running. So he had yanked loose all the wires. He just pulled everything.

"It's my fault she's having trouble with her motor," he said. "I should pay for that damage. I should get a new windshield too, I guess. I owe her a lot of money." He paused. "We've been through a lot together, Gram."

"Yes."

He was silent for a moment. Then he began talking again. He talked slowly, each word seeming to come from him as if it were a great weight which he had to lift from himself if he were to breathe again. And if I thought I had glimpsed his life before, now I truly saw it with a terrible clarity. Perhaps I should have been frightened by what he told me, but I wasn't. Instead, I was overwhelmed by a great pity and grief for the way heroin could entrap a gently bred boy so that he saw no way to escape from his own desperate acts, which in fact were only entangling him more. Methadone must save him, I thought. It must! It's been helping—some. That's why he's calmer. But it must save him altogether.

His voice broke in on my thought.

There was nothing he hadn't done, he was saying. He had cheated, lied, stolen to get money. Working hand in glove with girls he knew —girls who had jobs in department stores—he could get money easily, for customers would come in and carelessly lay down their handbags on the counter for a moment. That made it a snap. Through these girls he often got possession of credit cards. Then what a time he had had! He had gone to the most expensive nightclubs and eating places and theaters. He'd blown it for fair. He'd bought the necessary expensive clothes to appear in, of course, which later he'd sold when he needed money again. Oh, it had been fun—acting as if he owned the world! But it never lasted. And you could use a credit card only once. After it was reported it was no good to you. So then you had to do other things.

"What other things?" I asked when he paused. For I wanted to know it all.

And he told me. In that low, quiet voice, dragging it all up, freeing himself, he told me the rest. How he had held people up with the threat of his poised hunting knife until he was given the money he demanded. How he had robbed stores. How, in fact, he had broken and entered a private house once with another boy. They had cased the joint first, he said, and they knew the household routine, so they knew what to do and when to do it. After entering and threatening with the knife, they had tied up both the man and the woman and left them lying on the floor, gagged as well as bound, while they ransacked the place. The loot that time was prodigious. They got not only money but furs and jewelry and many small articles that were easy to sell. But they hadn't hurt either the man or the woman.

He stopped. Then—finally—he told me the last thing. It was of an encounter he had had in a place where he himself had been held up twice and had had to hand over the heroin just bought with money that had been so hard to come by. The third time he went there he had decided if he met that man again waiting for him at the foot of the stairs, he was going to fight. He was going to use his knife if he had to. There he paused a moment. Then he finished.

"I had to, Gram. Use it. But when I got outside I threw that knife down a manhole. And I thought I would never stop shaking. I thought I would *never* stop shaking."

I reached out my hand and took his in a warm tight clasp.

"Gregory," I said, "I knew long ago that you would have to go down this road till you got to the end of it. Are you there now, darling?"

"I'm all through with Harlem and the Bronx," he told me. "I never want to go there again. Never."

The rest of that Thanksgiving Day was indelibly imprinted on my memory. Gregory was tired after our long talk and said he wanted to take a nap, so he stretched out on his sofa. I went to my bedroom. After a while I heard him moving about and I went to join him. Neither of us was hungry after our big turkey dinner but I could see he was restless. Presently he told me he would have to go out for a short time.

Since he had let me in so far that afternoon, I ventured a question. "Where are you going, Gregory?"

"I'm going to Artie's, Gram."

"Why, darling?"

"I have to, Gram. I have to get some methadone. I haven't had any since this morning when we went to the clinic, and it's not open tonight because of the holiday. And I haven't any here and I need it. I have to have it, that's all."

"Where will you get it?"

"Artie may have some. He's been getting it for Ellen and me all the time. I told you the clinic didn't give me enough. I haven't been getting anything else though. Just methadone."

"Have you any money?"

"No."

"How will you pay Artie, then?"

"I don't know."

"Will he let you have it anyway?"

"I'm not sure. I owe him quite a lot now."

"If he won't give it to you, what will you do?"

"Don't worry, Gram."

That was all he said but it was enough, for I thought of all he had told me that afternoon earlier and my heart shook.

"How much will you need?"

"It's gone up in price lately. It's harder to get now. They're about five dollars apiece instead of three or four."

"I'll give you ten dollars, Gregory."

"You don't have to."

"I do have to."

Indeed I did have to, for I could not face the alternative. To be sure, Gregory no longer had his knife—I had seen to that—but he could break into a store and rob the till. He would take that chance, I knew, as he had taken a chance driving Artie's car. And if he was caught—everything undone. Everything. This was not to be endured—or even considered. No matter what Gregory's counselor had said about never giving him money. No matter at all.

"I will give you ten dollars, Gregory, if you will promise me you will get nothing but methadone with it."

"I promise, Gram. That's all I want."

It was dark outside now, a cold, raw, wet, and drizzling evening. I told him I would drive him to Edgewood and would wait somewhere while he went to Artie's house. I would wait in the business section, which was safer for me than going into the ghetto down the alley where Artie lived.

"If Artie doesn't have any, I know a couple of other people who might. But maybe it will take me quite a while to find them, Gram."

"All right. I'll wait half an hour for you. If you're not back by then, I'll go home."

It was so agreed and we set out. The streets were almost deserted because of the weather and the fact that it was Thanksgiving night and most people were with their families in their homes celebrating the holiday.

I decided to park in front of a big Woolworth store, and it was there Gregory left me. All up and down the avenue the stores were closed, of course, though lights burned dimly in the fronts of most of them as a protection against burglary. There had been a robbery of a jewelry store only the night before. The jeweler had been shot dead and also one of the robbers, but two others had escaped. As a consequence the town was edgy and police cars were regularly patrolling the area in the event of another robbery that night.

I made a note of the time as Gregory left me. He had no watch on him but he said he would know—and be back. "Don't worry." He thought Artie would have what he wanted, so he shouldn't be long.

His long figure slipped silently across the street and disappeared in the darkness. There was another car with no one in it parked opposite mine and I discovered two more further down the way. What were they doing there, I wondered? Since no stores were open and the theater was around the corner on another street, why were those cars there? Would they be suspect by the prowling police, I asked myself? Indeed, would I be suspect myself?

I could imagine a patrol on its rounds spotting me, an old woman sitting alone in my car with no lights on and no motor running. He would stop and ask me what I was doing there? And what would I say? What, indeed, could I say? I had no idea. There would be no reason, no sense, in any reply I might make. Not even the stores were open. Were there apartments above some of those stores where I might say my grandson was visiting? I was not sure—but there were certainly very few lights up there.

My uneasiness increased, so whenever a police car moved slowly past me down the avenue on its beat, I tried to slump out of sight behind my wheel, and when it had passed, I followed it after a moment and drove around the block out of its sight to come back and park in a slightly different spot. I did this several times, not at all sure what I was gaining and completely without emotion or any clear thought. I did not want to think. Not yet. What could I think anyway? But when the half hour had passed I returned to the same place where Gregory had left me.

He was not there. And he did not come. I waited ten minutes longer and then, as agreed, I drove home, because I had no idea when or even if he would get back to me. Something might have happened to him already, I told myself.

As I opened my door I heard my telephone ringing. It was Greg.

"*Gram!* Where *were* you? I went back to Woolworth's and you weren't *there!* Where *were* you?"

There was a note of sheer panic in his voice, and for the first time I realized sharply how completely Gregory was depending on me. I was the only sure hold he had on the life he was trying so desperately to straighten out, and he had thought I had deserted him. I spoke reassuringly.

"I came home, darling, because I had waited more than half an hour for you. But if you want me to come get you, I will. Did you have any luck?"

"No! That's the *thing!* I went everywhere but I couldn't get any. That's what took me so long! Listen, Gram! I was offered heroin. But I *resisted!* I wouldn't take it. I *resisted!*"

"Oh, Greg! Good for you! Where are you now?"

"I'm at an outside telephone booth in the alley near Artie's."

"Shall I pick you up at the monument?"

"Yes."

I found him there waiting for me. He was tense, his movements jerky.

"Gram, I've got to have something. If I can't get methadone, grass will do. But I've got to have that. See! Here's the money you gave me. Here it is, like I told you. I still have it. But I've got to get grass! If I only had some grass I'd be okay."

"Do you know where you can get some?"

He did. It was at a place up the river. He knew two boys who always had it. They were rich. They'd made a pile selling drugs because their father was rich and had staked them to some capital to start. They were fixed well. He knew they'd have it. "Grass is better than heroin, Gram. Grass doesn't harm you. I know it's illegal, but I don't want to go back onto heroin."

"I don't want you to. Tell me how to get to this place where the two boys are."

I did not understand his terrible craving. I had never experienced it or anything like it. I only knew it was real and that we were at a crisis, and I had no choice but to do what I did.

So I drove through the night up to a luxurious setup along the river. The parking area was huge, but even so it was hard to find a slot for my car. We went around and around until at last I slid into an opening.

I turned off my motor. Ahead of me about a quarter of a mile away I could see the enormous brilliantly lit pile of the apartment building. Gregory had told me it had its own police force and no one would bother me. This was the safest place to go for grass, or in fact for anything. I needn't worry.

"I'll wait half an hour for you, Greg, as I did before. No longer. If you aren't back then, I'll go home."

He knew I would. And he knew it was a long way for him to walk. "I'll be back," he said, as he slipped out of the car.

I watched him as he moved toward the distant lighted entrance to be swallowed up and disappear behind the doors there. I was cold so I turned on my motor to get some heat. But mostly I sat in the dark cold silence alone with my thoughts.

I asked myself—What was I doing in a situation like this? What in the world was I doing? In the numbed confusion of my mind and my emotions I found no clear answer. Yet the question persisted. It had been imprisoned within me and I had held it there, refusing to give it room. Now, in my solitude, it pushed its way up and out. It caught me—held me—made me shiver in a helplessness I had never known before.

The time that passed was both too long and too short as the blackness around me grew blacker. I heard Gregory before I saw him. He was fumbling at the door and slid in beside me with a sigh of triumphant relief.

"I got it, Gram! I stayed just long enough to smoke one joint. Then I left. I've spent all the ten dollars. But I've got enough grass for myself now for several days and some left over that I can sell. That's good, Gram! We won't have to worry for a while."

We.

I reached out and started my motor but I made no reply. I thought again—What am I doing here? What in the world am I *doing* here? And the answer—like lightning through the darkness within me—came clear and sharp, as dangerous, as devastating: *You have been an accomplice in an act that is against the law.*

"Gram? Gram! Why don't you start? Are you all right?"

I drew a great breath. "Yes—no—*yes.* Oh, Gregory, listen! I've just now seen—I've just now understood—this whole evening has been all wrong, darling! Absolutely all *wrong*. I wanted to help you. I tried to. I thought I was. But I really haven't helped you at all."

"But you *have*, Gram!"

"No. I've only pushed you further down the hill. Made it easier for you to go that way. And in so doing—don't you understand?—I, myself, have gone down hill too, against everything I've always known and believed and lived by. My whole *life*. I don't know yet quite how it happened. I thought I was doing right. I thought I *had* to. But I—well —I just wasn't *thinking*. I was only feeling." I paused. "Gregory darling, what I'm saying is that I can never again—*never*—do anything like this with you or for you, no matter how much I love you. Tonight —for me—has not been a beginning. It's been an end."

Gregory was silent for a long moment. Then—"Gram? Don't worry. I think I know how you feel. And thanks anyway."

That night, alone in my bedroom, I went over it all once more. Indeed no, I had not helped my grandson. I had only supported him in his craving for drugs. His counselor at the clinic had been right. Helping that way wasn't any good.

What was? What else—what different—could I do?

I stared into the darkness and—as earlier that evening in the car —I felt a complete helplessness overwhelm me. For I couldn't answer. I didn't know. I didn't *know!* All my life I had been so sure, so confident, that I could find ways to do what I set out to do—what I had figured out was right to do—

What *I* had figured out. *I,* alone.

Prideful. That's what I had been. Yes, prideful. *Arrogant.*

I did not like the word. I did not like my thought. But I lay very still facing it, accepting it. Then I put my clasped hands together in a silent prayer and spoke to that God to whom, long years ago, I had pledged only praise.

"God, I don't know. I just don't *know*. Please help me find what to do. Because I don't know—and I need help. *Please,* God!"

It was strange to be talking that way. For He was still a distant God to me. No nearer than that day I had joined the church. But—humbly —I hoped He had heard.

12

Be not deceived; God is not mocked: for whatsoever a man soweth, that shall he also reap.

Galatians 6:7

Things changed after that. For, following the holiday, Ellen's car, finally put in shape, had become operative, and since that was so and since some kind of truce had been established between her and her father, she was expected to live at her own home again. This was not altogether pleasing to her, as it meant separation from Gregory. When she pointed out to him that it was only fair for him to take his turn at staying with her parents, he was not pleased either. He did not feel comfortable with them. If he went, he said, it would be for just a weekend. After that they would have to divide their time between the two places. But he would go there only weekends, when her father would be away most of the time on the golf course.

The first time they left me I sank into a chair after they had gone, filled with the strangest feeling. How long since I had been alone? How long since I had not keyed myself to their imminent return and whatever they might need of me? It seemed ages. I had lost track of much through those chaotic days. I had just lived from one tense moment to the next. But now I was alone and I would be alone all day, all tonight, and most of tomorrow. I could let my solitude enfold me. But above all else, I could *clean.*

I looked about my big living room. There were fluffs of gray under the sofa, crumbs on the carpet, shiny bits of foil from cigarette wrappings caught in chairs and full ashtrays everywhere. The window shades were askew. Dust was thick on my lovely antique table in the dinette just beyond. The sofa itself was still a bed with tumbled blankets in a heap because I had said I would change the sheets in their absence.

I rose and went into my kitchen. But I knew full well what I would find there. A sticky floor. Long hairs in the sink. Grease spots on the wall above the stove, and that itself encrusted with spilled food. Blackened pots and pans, a disordered silver drawer, and dishes out of place. Theoretically they had cleaned up after their haphazard eating, but it was superficial cleaning. And long ago I had given up trying to keep the place as I was accustomed to keeping it. By comparison with other things this was not important. So I had simply overlooked the mess when I went there to snatch my own meals. There just wasn't time enough anyway, for we lived in a constant rush from here to there every day. Nor would I hassle them about it. My standards were not theirs, and in their minds they were doing all right.

Well, the stove would have to wait until I could take it all apart and let the parts soak. But I could at least mop my kitchen floor and use my vacuum cleaner and make up the sofa bed and straighten the shades and dust everywhere and so bring some neatness back to the place.

As I worked I thought how completely those two young people had taken over my apartment. I was paying the rent, but they—my two guests—were living in more of it than I was. The living room with the TV was entirely theirs, the kitchen was theirs whenever they wanted it, and they preempted the bathroom with thoughts only of their own needs. I told myself with faint amusement that I was like the hired girl of years ago who had no place to call her own except the third-floor back bedroom. Well, thank goodness I had the back bedroom —most of the time! And all this would be worthwhile if— If what? If God worked the miracle I had not been able to bring about. For it was up to God now, I told myself. Had He heard my appeal? I hoped so. Oh, I hoped so!

When the two of them had left me that weekend they had both completed their nine-day detox program and they had said that when Ellen's car brought them back on Monday they would go straight to the clinic and ask to be put on "maintenance." If they could be enrolled on maintenance there would be no more need to get methadone by hook or by crook, as their doses then would be what they required. So everything would be legal and this was what Gregory wanted.

But they were both rejected. And they were in a furious turmoil when they told me this. When I asked the natural question—*Why?*—Gregory exploded. "Because we're too *young!* Because only people in their twenties are accepted! Your *age* shouldn't matter! It's your *need* that's important! But the doctor wouldn't agree that I needed as much as I told him I did! He never *has* believed me! Never—from the beginning! And the thing is that I only need a *little* now. Only a *little*. But if I'm not going to be allowed to get that little—" He broke off.

Gregory, tense and enraged over this refusal, this dashing of his hopes and plans, was in a reckless mood. What would he do? What *wouldn't* he do? Where was God in this matter? I couldn't wait to find out, so I betook myself to Mrs. Kirk's office for advice, first sending up a prayer that this was right for me to do and hoping—believing —it was. As his counselor, she had been interested in Gregory from the start. I told her I had come to see her because Gregory had not made it clear to me just why he had been turned down. Was it really because of his youth? Was age, not need, the criterion for admission to maintenance? Could she explain?

She could and she did. Their funds, their staff, their space in that old building, and their time—especially their time, for all of them were volunteers—all these were limited. They really worked on a shoestring. Only a certain number of patients could be taken care of, so it had been decided that those needing maintenance care the most were those who had been on drugs the longest. That meant the older ones. They were usually in their twenties.

"And Gregory is nineteen," I said. "I see. But couldn't he repeat the nine-day program? It might work a second time."

No, he could not, she told me, as she had told me once before. It was not allowed. There were too many applicants waiting their turn. It wouldn't be fair. "Each one has to sink or swim on his first try," she said. "That is the rule—and they know it. I'm sorry."

"Well, but if one of the older men should drop out—?"

"The same rule holds. Besides, the doctor's decision is irrevocable. Final." She paused. "I'm sorry," she repeated. "I know Gregory has real possibilities. I believed in him. I still do. And I wish him luck." She paused again. And I felt a relenting kindness in her. She would really like to help, I thought. I thought too that she was remembering all those hours when I, an elderly, weary, limping old grandmother, a monument of patience, waited for my grandson in those three small crowded rooms, sitting sometimes on top of a table because no empty chairs were available. She said, "Why don't you try the county hospital? It's a much bigger setup than here. Better run. Longer established. And it's no further from where you live than this town. Hundreds of boys go there. I'll give you the name of a social worker. I'll call him for you first. He's a good friend of mine and owes me a favor. He'll do what he can."

I was immensely grateful. *Thank You, God!* This, then, had been right for me to do. God had shown me the way.

I took Gregory to the county hospital the very next afternoon. (Ellen had gone shopping with her mother.) It was a huge place and modern in every respect. I was pleased with what I saw—the large spotless area where there were plenty of chairs for visitors ranged against the wall and a table full of magazines to while away the waiting period. (There had been nothing at all at the other clinic.) I was impressed too by the brisk-stepping white-uniformed nurses, the prompt courteous answer given my question at the desk. Yes, we could see Mr. Foster. He was expecting us. He would be free soon. Would we be seated?

We saw him in about half an hour and he came directly to the point. The only way to get on the maintenance program there, he said, would be for Gregory to enroll as a patient and live in the hospital for three weeks behind locked doors in the wing given over to this purpose. At that my heart sank, for Gregory's spirit was too wild and undisciplined to be caged like that. I had thought he could go over every day as he had at Milltown, and I could not imagine his accepting such a prisonlike sentence. But to my surprise, he had already learned of this requirement and had made up his mind to accept it. Yet when he expressed his willingness to do just that and asked how soon he might come, Mr. Foster shook his head.

"My dear boy, we have a waiting list of more than fifty names, and accommodations for only seventeen or eighteen. You won't be able to get in here for six months or more."

Gregory shot to his feet. *"Six months!* How do I live till then? How do I *live?* Tell me that!" And he flung himself out through the door.

I followed silently, after a word of thanks to Mr. Foster. What was the answer? Gregory didn't know. Nor did I. The clinics were doing their best but it still wasn't enough. And it was illegal for a doctor to supply him with what he needed. So here was this boy, "clean" at the moment and passionately wanting to stay that way legally, yet he could get no assistance anywhere. What would he do? I was fearful. I was terribly fearful.

That night I sent up another of my supplicating prayers that was more urgent than any earlier ones. *God! Are You there? Are You somewhere in the wild blue yonder? If You are, please help us! Please, please help us now! We need it! And I don't know. I still don't know at all—*

I heard no answer. I was given no intimation or feeling of what to do. Not this time. Only silence came back from that high blue void.

Gregory was now going to Ellen's for more than just a weekend. Twice he was there during the middle of the week and the next thing I knew he had given up his job at the church. He could not, he told me, get back from Ellen's in time to suit Moe. He was invariably late and that angered Moe, who was going to get one of the college boys now returning to town for the Christmas holidays as a replacement for Gregory. He shrugged off my shocked disappointment, saying there just wasn't enough money in the job anyway, and never had been. All this made me most uncomfortable—for Moe, the business manager, and the minister had all been most tolerant throughout the entire time with Gregory. But all I could do was write notes of appreciation to each one, expressing my thanks and my regrets for such an ending.

In my heart I knew why this had happened. Having a car again, Ellen and Gregory could now travel far and wide hunting for—and getting—the methadone they needed. This took time. It also took money—and they knew of only one fast way to get that. It was a vicious circle, portending no good. And I was helpless. All I could do was watch and wait. And hope. And pray.

For what?

For God's miracle.

But there was none. Nor any sign of one. Not to me. And I was shaken.

I don't know just when I discovered that my apartment was no longer the home for Gregory and Ellen that it had been in the beginning. I noticed first that the crowd had changed. Familiar faces were absent, while new ones from the area where Ellen lived had appeared. These young people were not like the first group. These regarded me with suspicion and considered me an intruder. When they came in they gave me the briefest nod—if indeed they noticed me at all. And they gathered together in low-voiced conferences in my kitchen at the telephone there or they huddled together with their backs to me in a corner. So I left the room.

Yes, things had changed. My apartment was now nothing but a home base. A place where Ellen and Gregory could keep their clothes. A place to which they could come any time of night or day. A rendezvous for their companions. A point of departure for sudden secret mysterious flights to—I never knew where or what for. Or a place simply for sleeping.

I was being used as I had said once I would not be used. Yet how could I help it? Without hassling? Without—as a result of that hassling—sending Gregory (and Ellen too, of course) back to Artie's again? Where else would they go? Ellen's parents would not have them there. Her father did not like Gregory, would never consent to such an arrangement. Nor would the two of them go even if they were asked. Certainly not Gregory. And his own parents had said long ago they must marry if they hoped to be welcomed there by Fern and Tom.

I felt as though I had a tiger by the tail. One I could neither tame nor let go. How was this going to be resolved? I had no idea. If God were with me, as I had believed He was, where had He gone? I felt deserted—and very alone.

The two of them had dashed in last night and dashed out again this morning. They had given me only a few words but they had left soiled dishes, clothes dropped here and there, drawers half open, and one high-heeled green platform shoe sticking out of the closet door. Where they were going I did not know. Or when they would be back. It suddenly didn't matter whether I knew or not. I was tired. I was tense and tired and edgy and deeply worried. Gregory had gone out of my reach. He had gone a long way from me. He was a stranger. And Ellen had him. Ellen with her car and her long hungry loving arms. And there was nothing I could do to bring him back. So thinking, I sank into my wing chair and let the stillness engulf me.

Yet I could not relax. My earlier thought that I could manage by myself returned to mock me now. It was true that I had never corrected, advised, criticized—that, instead, I had accepted. And my door had always opened to their call or need. But no more. They no longer called. They had no need. Not of me. They hardly noticed me, actually. I would tidy up around my apartment soon and they would return when it suited them, never aware of the tidying up. So there would be no appreciative thanks—nor would help, of course, have been given to that end.

Times had changed indeed.

Yes, times had changed. And I stopped praying for help, for it did no good. And there was no longer anything to be thankful for, so I stopped praying entirely. I just waited.

The days passed and I grew used to seeing Gregory as someone I had not known or seen before. Gregory stumbling in high, talking and laughing loudly. Or Gregory drunk, his eyes dull and heavy, his speech thick and uncertain. Gregory, on the heights or in the depths. I never knew how it would be. But never anymore was he quiet and happy as he had been at Thanksgiving time.

No, Gregory now was tense and desperate and totally indifferent to any word from me. He must be using more than methadone, I thought, or he wouldn't be like this. But I could not bear to think that so I pushed the thought away.

My only hope—indeed our only hope (for Fern and Tom knew how matters were going)—was the county hospital. And a frail hope it was. For how could that long waiting list be circumvented? Nevertheless, as if it could be, Fern had made inquiries regarding the cost of those three required weeks of confinement, and she and Tom had both said they were willing and ready to meet it at any time.

I told Gregory this. It was nothing but a straw for him to clutch at but I thought he needed that straw, and indeed when I saw the small spark of hope leap into his face, even though it quickly died, I was glad I had spoken. Ellen, however, was not pleased at the possibility, no matter how distant. For her parents, who had also investigated, as Fern had, declared flatly that they would never meet this expense.

"Because it maybe doesn't cure you anyway," Ellen said to me.

"The doctors don't guarantee it will. Besides, my folks don't think I need it."

I was inclined to agree. More than once I had seen Ellen clear-eyed when Gregory was in a daze. I suspected sometimes that she had not helped him resist temptation on occasions when she might have, for she had told me once that when he was high she could always get him to do what she wanted. "I like him best that way," she had said. "Then he's more affectionate." Ellen, I had learned, was astute—as Gregory was not—and she acted on reason, whereas he was all un-thinking impulse. With these weapons she managed him.

She had other weapons too. She had her car (which she never permitted him to drive) and she still had her unemployment check coming in regularly. His income, dependent on drug sales which always held an element of danger and so often fell apart, was uncer-tain. But all this control which she could exert gave rise in him to resentment. More and more I could see it—hear it—in their quarrels. Sometimes he would fling away and out and be gone for hours at a stretch. And this absence was *his* weapon, since it made her unsure of his love for her. Would he come back? How strong was her hold on him? How far could she push him? She must be careful.

And then came the day when I heard Gregory speaking too loudly, too angrily over the telephone. "But I tell you I *didn't* take your money! It was somebody else! No, it was *not* me! But I know—I can explain—" Then the phone banged down. He rushed from the kitchen and spoke hurriedly to Ellen in a low voice before he rushed out. She said, "He has to fix something—a misunderstanding—" And she followed him.

It was the next day in the evening when the phone rang again. I was alone. I heard Ellen's mother's voice. She was glad Ellen wasn't there. She wanted to talk just to me, even though she didn't know how to say what she had to tell. Maybe she was all wrong but she was afraid she wasn't. The thing was that she had been away all day yesterday, the house had been shut up and locked, and when she came back she found someone had been there. Ellen, naturally, had a key. So it had been Ellen. Ellen and, of course, Gregory. She was sure it was they because she had found Ellen's scarf dropped on the floor upstairs, where it hadn't been when she herself had left. And she had picked up one of Gregory's gloves out in the driveway. They were the ones who had been there and taken the silver. She wasn't sure, of course, for she had no real proof. But she knew they needed money. They always needed money. And Ellen's father had said that because of the insurance the loss must be reported. Anyway, would I please look around my apartment and see if—among their things—I could find any—

I said I would. Then I hung up the receiver.

Gregory was doing everything he had done on heroin. Maybe he was really on it again, as I had not wanted to believe. Even now I didn't know for sure. All I knew for sure was that if he was on it, then no one was safe. No one at all. Least of all Gregory.

Gregory, whom I had undertaken to rescue. Gregory, whom I loved better than my life. Gregory, who was helpless in the grip of an evil which made it impossible for him to help himself.

And there was no one to help him. Not even God anymore. He had not heard my calls for help. Perhaps I had waited too long. Perhaps His ears were not attuned to hearing me ask. Anyway, silence had been my only answer. So, because I couldn't do just nothing at all, I was thrown back, I thought, on my own resources again.

13

And all this assembly shall know that the Lord saveth not with sword and spear: for the battle is the Lord's. . . .

1 Samuel 17:47

It was the next day after Ellen's mother had phoned me and once again I was in Mrs. Kirk's office. This had been the only thing I could think of to do. She had not wanted to see me. She had told me over the telephone that she could do no more for me than she had already done with her introduction to Mr. Foster. But when I said, "Mrs. Kirk, I ask for only five minutes. Only five minutes! That's all. But I must have those," the urgency of my tone persuaded her to yield.

I faced her across her desk and came straight to the point. My voice shook. I could not help it. And perhaps it was as well, for it added to the pressure I wanted to put on her. Exactly what I said I cannot now remember, but it went like this:

"Mrs. Kirk, I'm here because I'm at the end of my rope. I can't carry on any longer. There is nothing more I can do and I'm exhausted. But if I send Gregory away, where will he go? I'll tell you. He'll go to the devil. He'll be lost. Lost to the world, to me, to our family—and lost to himself. He'll be *lost*, Mrs. Kirk—and that will be on my conscience, because I ought to be able to find a way to save him. But"—I leaned toward her—"it will be on your conscience too. Unless you will help me again. You've got to help me, because there's no one else. You've got to help me get Gregory into the county hospital right away. Not in a few weeks. Not even next week. But sooner than that. Now. *Today.*" I steadied myself, my hands gripped together. I must finish. I must say all I'd planned to say before my five minutes was up. I went on.

"I know there are always exceptions made to all rules in urgent situations. I *know* that. You know it too. Well, this is an urgent situation, Mrs. Kirk. Because I can't go on and there's no one else. Except you, Mrs. Kirk. Except you. And you have a conscience. You care too. You know Gregory mustn't be lost—" Against my best efforts a sob rose in my throat and my last words were choked. "Will you please—*please*—do something to get Gregory into the county hospital right away?"

I stopped. That was the gist of it. That was the heart of it. Rules could be broken. Something could be done. Something must be done —and she was the one to do it. She had connections at the county hospital because of her work. She knew people in authority there. Hadn't she already given me a name? She could give another. She must—because Mr. Foster hadn't helped. But someone else could. She could go above him—right to the top.

Watching her, holding my breath, I waited. I knew my time was up and I had said it all. All there was to say. There was nothing more to add. At last she spoke, her words coming slowly.

"I can see," she said, "I can see you've reached your limit. And— yes—you're right. If you let Gregory go, he will really be lost. He's at his last stand. And I don't want him to fall either, Mrs. Randall. As you said, I have a conscience." She fell silent for a moment.

"I don't know what I can do. Or if I can do anything. But I'll try. Today is Thursday. Give me a few days—say a week—" She was silent again. "I'll try," she repeated. "But don't phone me. Don't try to get in touch with me to ask anything. If I have any news for you, my secretary will call you. I—I really can't promise a thing. You understand? All I can do is try." She rose.

I rose, too. "Thank you," I said. "Thank you very much." And I left her.

Never, never will I forget that day—the rest of it. It was as memorable as Thanksgiving had been.

I went back to my apartment. Ellen and Gregory were both there. He was cleaning his boots. I remembered then that when they had come in last night—or, rather, early this morning about four o'clock —they had tracked in mud.

"We were in the country," Gregory had said to me. "We were walking in the country in a muddy field."

What had they been doing walking in a muddy field long after midnight? Burying the things they had stolen from Ellen's father's house? Or digging them up from their hiding place to take to some buyer of stolen goods for the money they wanted? It was a passing flashing thought which I dismissed because I didn't know. And there was no use harboring such an idea. No use at all. But it was a possibility.

They cleaned their boots and scraped up the mud from my rugs. Then Gregory said he was going out again. He went alone. Ellen stretched out on the sofa with a book. I retired to my bedroom. Gregory would be back soon, Ellen had said. And then they had a date to go somewhere. He was just going to Artie's. That was all. He would not be long.

Time passed, however, and he did not return. Ellen went to the kitchen to get herself something to eat. She ate much more than Gregory did. It was another way I knew she used fewer drugs than he, for Gregory, on drugs, ate hardly anything at all. I called out to her and asked her please to clean up when she was finished and she said she would. Presently she went back to her reading.

More time passed. I was uneasy and went out to ask Ellen if she was, too. No, she said. He would be back any minute now. He was getting some methadone and it was increasingly difficult to lay your hands on any. "Probably Artie was out of it and he's scouting around all over Edgewood."

I accepted her explanation but for some unaccountable reason I was still very uneasy. It was late in the afternoon before I heard Ellen let Gregory in. I heard his voice, very low, saying something. Then I heard her wail.

"Gregory! You *didn't!* Oh, why did you go *there? Now* what do you think *I'll* do? That was *my* money! You know it was! All of it! How do you think I'm going to get along without any money till my next check comes in? How do you think— Oh, I could *kill* you for being so stupid!"

I went to join them. They were standing facing each other, Gregory with an angry, defeated, guilty, desperate look on his face.

"I couldn't help it," he said. "There was none in Edgewood. None at all. I had to go to New York. And I didn't have my knife so I couldn't help it when four or five of them jumped on me. I didn't have my knife—or anything. Well, now I owe you twenty dollars."

He was beaten. It was in his voice and on his face. I had never seen him so beaten. I went back to my bedroom to the table I had set up there as my desk. I kept my checkbook on it and my handbag. A moment later I returned to the living room with a ten-dollar bill in my hand and a check.

"Here's half of what Gregory owes you, Ellen," I said, holding out the bill. (After all, I had taken his knife.) "It's all I have right now. But here's a check for the other half."

She took them both without a word. Gregory said nothing either. I couldn't be sorry he hadn't had his knife. No, I couldn't be sorry about that. I left them alone together and returned to my room once more. I heard their voices but nothing of what they said. I only knew by the sound that Ellen was unforgiving. All I could think was that Gregory had, after all, returned to his old haunts in the city, although he had said he never wanted to go there again.

After a while I heard the front door open and close. Had they both gone out on their date? I went to see. But Gregory was there alone.

"Ellen's gone home," he said. "She's mad at me." He turned on his radio, flung himself on his sofa, which he had opened up into a bed, and I knew he wanted to be left by himself.

I don't know how much later it was—perhaps in the early evening —when I asked Gregory if I could get him something to eat, for he had had nothing since breakfast. No, he didn't want anything, he said. So I had a bite myself and then I joined him in the living room. Gregory was flat on his back, his hands twitching on his chest.

"I haven't any methadone. I haven't any money. And I haven't any grass. I might as well be dead. I'd be better off dead. I wish I was dead."

That was the beginning of a dreadful two hours. Gregory, with his hands now gripping the sofa top, pulled himself as far up as he could get and began talking. He talked and he talked as he had on Thanksgiving Day. And all the time he talked he kept pulling himself up and down on the sofa until he could pull himself no higher up, for there was nothing for him to get a hold on. I thought of that expression "climbing the wall," for that was exactly what Gregory was trying to do. He was at an extremity—physically, mentally, and spiritually— with no help for himself. Unless talking to me was a help. I didn't know if it was or would be, but I sat down beside him ready to listen anyway, and hoping that he would find some relief in words from the suffering I could see he was enduring.

"My head aches," he said. "I feel sick."

I got him to open his shirt and roll over on his stomach so I could massage his neck and bare back. And somehow during my steady ministrations I understood that he had come back to me from the place to which he had withdrawn. For I was in his confidence again.

"You think I don't worry about anything," he said. "Everybody thinks I don't worry about anything because I keep telling other people not to. But I do worry. I worry all the time. That's why I can't sleep."

"What are you worrying about now, darling? Tell me."

"About all the money I owe. I owe everybody money. Everybody!"

This anxiety had been building up in him. Building and building. I had heard it in his voice over the phone. I had felt it driving him —driving him—

"I never seem to get ahead," he was saying. "I keep trying—"

My hands went on rhythmically over his back. I answered quietly, "I'm glad to know what's troubling you, Greg. I'm glad you're telling me. I said to you once you need never be afraid to tell me anything. Except a lie. Now tell me more. Tell me all you owe everybody, one at a time. Tell me. Then we'll talk about how you can get your debts paid off. Because it can be done, you know. You can do it. I'll help you. It may take time. It *will*. But we'll work it out together, darling. You're not alone in this."

We sat there, with me talking when he wasn't, sharing his burden with him, rubbing his back and neck and talking—talking—till presently I felt him relaxing, growing calmer. I went to the kitchen then and brought him a cup of beef broth and a plate of toast.

"Drink this soup, Greg. And eat the toast. It will taste good."

"Money!" he said, when the soup and toast were gone. "It's at the bottom of everything. All my troubles. It's always been. If I just had money I'd be all right."

I gave a soft little laugh. It was time to laugh, I thought. "If you just knew how to *handle* money, you mean," I said. "But now listen to me for a minute, because I have news for you."

Until then I had not been sure whether to tell him of my visit to

Mrs. Kirk earlier in the day. I did not want to raise any false hopes but I decided that he was in desperate need of hope—some rope to which he might cling—and this time, I told myself, it was a little more than a straw.

He listened tensely, his eyes fixed on mine.

"Nothing's certain," I reminded him as I finished.

He drew a long slow breath. "No. I know. But I have a feeling. I have a good feeling I'll get there. And Gram, when I'm through there —when I'm out and all right and get my methadone every day—all I need—" He drew another breath. "Think, Gram! All I have to do is go get it! They tell you to come early in the morning so you can go from the hospital to whatever job you have. And I'll *get* one, Gram! I'll get one and begin right off paying my debts. Do you hear me?"

"I hear you, darling. It's a wonderful plan. Hold on to it."

"Money!" he said in a low voice. "Money!"

"Don't forget it's *just* money, Greg. Only good if you know what to do with it."

"Yeah. I know."

That night I thought—Now it's really up to God. Mrs. Kirk—and God. And I prayed for forgiveness for my doubts and I asked for help once again. And then I thanked Him for Gregory's return to me once more.

14

. . . and if I perish, I perish.

Esther 4:16

Ellen came back the next day repentantly, bringing methadone, generously forgiving Gregory for losing her money, her long arms reaching out for him greedily. Gregory had told her at once of his new hope, and I could see she did not like the news at all.

"Would you really go—if you got the chance?" she asked.

"Yes! I told you. It's what I want."

"But I'll be without you a whole month!"

"Not quite that long."

"Long enough. I can't bear it! Oh, Gregory! Don't leave me! Please don't leave me for as long as that!" She began to cry and I went out to them.

"Ellen, this may not happen. We won't know surely for another week. But it's a move that everyone thinks is best for Gregory. His parents, Mrs. Kirk, and I—and he too thinks so. You say you love him. Why, then, don't you, like the rest of us, want what is best for him?"

She was silenced for only a moment. "You'll spend all that money and it may not do any good at all. Sometimes it doesn't."

"It's not your money, Ellen. Why should you worry?"

"It isn't that I'm worrying about. If I could just go too—but I can't."

I thought the next few days would never end. The waiting was almost intolerable. My prayers were constant, though incoherent. I did not believe as wholly as I had earlier—and hope was not as supportive as belief. But I prayed anyway. I hated to go out anywhere lest I miss the ring of the telephone. I had left Fern's number as well as mine with Mrs. Kirk's secretary, but Fern heard nothing either.

The weekend dragged by for me. Ellen and Gregory were off somewhere but not at her home. They had not gone there since her mother had telephoned me that night. I had reported to her that I had found nothing in my apartment or among their things, and there I dropped the matter. There wasn't anything more for me to do. Anyway, I was certain that Gregory and Ellen had not gone there now. There were, however, plenty of other places to which they could betake themselves. One friend had a summer place by a lake. They might be there. So I was alone when the telephone rang on Monday morning.

"Mrs. Randall? This is Mrs. Kirk's secretary. Mrs. Kirk has asked me to tell you that if you will take Gregory to the county hospital a week from today—Monday next, at seven-thirty in the morning—he will be interviewed by Dr. Bennett. He is the chief of the department that interests you, and there is a chance—just a chance—that he may be willing to admit Gregory at once. Perhaps I should say almost at once. Certainly before Christmas."

Could I believe it? Tears flooded up and I could hardly reply to express my sincere thanks. "Please tell Mrs. Kirk that Gregory and I will definitely be at the county hospital next week Monday at seven thirty—and I can't thank her enough." Breathlessly then I relayed the news to Fern. She would have to go with us for that interview, because —in case he was accepted immediately—she, as the parent, must sign him in. I had no such authority. I could hardly wait for Gregory to come back so I could tell him. At the same time I worried about the condition he might be in. I never knew what to expect. And after a weekend away—

But he was all right. Neither high nor drunk. He walked in soberly and took my news in the same quiet way, saying only, "I'll believe this when I get there."

Ellen spoke up then. "But—*next* Monday? Why, Gregory, we have a big date over the weekend! Have you forgotten?" She turned to me. "Nick's folks are to be away so we'll have the whole house. All our crowd will be there. We're to go on Saturday afternoon and stay over. We can't miss it!"

"We'll come home Sunday," Gregory said, looking first at Ellen and then at me. "Sunday afternoon we'll be back."

I nodded. Ellen said no more. But I did. I turned to her and spoke pleasantly. "Ellen, since Gregory's appointment with the doctor is so early on Monday morning—at seven-thirty—I won't ask you to stay over with us Sunday night. I'm sure that after your weekend party Gregory will need sleep and a good rest." I smiled at her—"I'm just telling you so you won't plan to be here. I'm taking Gregory's mother with us that morning but no one else."

"Oh," she said. "I wouldn't expect to stay. After being away this last weekend—and again most of the next too—I'll have to go home, of course. My folks will expect me."

Somehow the rest of that week went by. I lived tensely. The impossible was coming to pass. It really was! Within me belief in the Lord returned and with it a shame for my doubts. Even so—the moment was not yet. And I held my breath, for I was anxious about this last party that was to come. There was danger there. Then I reminded myself that Gregory had come back all right from the last affair. Surely, now that so much was at stake—now that he knew of his chances—he would be careful. He would not take any risks.

Through the next few days Ellen and Gregory came and went. I asked no questions. They were late only once—Thursday. That night I let them both in at two o'clock. Then, to my surprise, Ellen departed at once to go to her own home. She said she wanted to get a party dress for the coming Saturday night. I looked at Gregory—but he was all right. Only terribly tired and—it seemed to me—depressed. Was something wrong? What could be?

I learned Friday morning when I went to the kitchen to get my own breakfast. I tiptoed past Gregory's bed and saw him wide awake. This was surprising—but even more so was it to see him pulling himself to a sitting position and hear him say what he did.

"I can't go to the hospital with you on Monday morning after all, Gram. I can't meet that doctor."

I stood stock-still. I couldn't believe what I had heard. "But everything's arranged! You're practically *there!* Practically in! Admitted!" I was sure of it. I was sure that at this point we were not going to be turned away. There might be a delay of a day or two but—I moved over to him and sat down in my big chair beside the sofa bed. "Gregory! What makes you say that?"

"Because Ellen's pregnant. I have to get a job and make a hundred and fifty so she can get an abortion."

I was simply stunned. Then reason came to my aid. "Gregory, I just don't believe that."

"It's true, Gram. She's had the rabbit test."

But I knew it wasn't true. This was her last desperate effort to keep him with her. I hardly heard what he was saying. This had to be done right away, he was telling me. She couldn't wait the three weeks he would be at the hospital. It wouldn't be safe then to have it done. It would be too late. Too dangerous. Now was the time. She had been going to a clinic in a town next to where she lived. She had been on a detox program there, one he himself could not get into because he didn't live in that area. And when she had become suspicious of her condition, a nurse there had given her the rabbit test. There was no doubt about it. "It's true," he repeated.

I told him I still didn't believe it. Was it possible that this boy, so wise in the ways of evil, so cynical, was really as guileless as he seemed? But I knew too how loyal he was and had always been, how indebted to Ellen, how gentle his nature was. These things tied him. I repeated I still did not believe it. I told him that this was an old ploy. As old as time itself. A trick used to trap a man—usually into marriage. What Ellen was trying to do was keep him from going into the hospital. He heard me out, his face immovable, his eyes great burning holes in it. I knew he was suffering tortures. When I finished, he said slowly, "If I thought she was trying to get a hundred and fifty dollars from me for—*nothing*—I'd wring her neck." He fell silent. Presently he went on. "You mustn't tell anybody this, Gram. She made me promise I wouldn't tell you. But I had to. You had to have a reason. Only you mustn't tell anybody else. She would be furious."

I did not reply. But as soon as I was alone, I called up Fern. She did not believe the story either. We talked the matter over awhile and came to some decisions. Then I hung up.

Saturday afternoon early Ellen appeared in the long evening dress she had gone home to get. It was pale green, and with her dark red hair she looked lovely. I greeted her with my planned speech about which Gregory knew nothing.

"Ellen," I said, "Gregory has told me you are pregnant. Frankly,

I don't believe it. But if you are, and if you think Gregory is going to miss this chance of getting into the county hospital because you want an abortion, you are mistaken. I have talked this over with Gregory's parents and with yours too, and we feel that Gregory is no more responsible for this happening than you are. So your parents and Gregory's parents have decided that the expense—if one is really necessary—will be divided between your two families. Gregory is going with me to the hospital on Monday morning for a seven-thirty appointment, just as planned."

Whatever she was thinking or feeling did not show on her face. She only said quickly—laughingly—"Why! I'm not pregnant! I only said I was for a joke'! I *told* Gregory I was just fooling! Don't you remember, Gregory?"

He turned his head and looked at her for a long moment. Then he said slowly, "No. I don't remember your saying that to me. I don't remember it at all."

"Oh, you forget a lot of things, Gregory. You know you do."

They left for their party. At the outside door, I reminded them both that when they returned on Sunday afternoon Ellen was not staying overnight.

"Oh, no!" she agreed. "I know I'm not. I have to go home. I promised my parents."

Gregory stumbled into my apartment on Sunday afternoon with Ellen supporting him. He hardly knew where he was and certainly not what he was doing. Ellen said lightly, "He's higher than a kite. I tried to stop him but—" She shrugged. "You know how he is when his mind gets made up. I'll stay a little while till he's better. Then I'll go."

I nodded and went to my bedroom, thinking he had time to sleep this off. But Ellen stayed more than a little while, and off and on I heard him speaking. Then I heard her voice going on and on. An hour or so later I heard them both laughing, then their voices again, then the radio. I called out the hour to Ellen. She said yes, she knew. But there was a show on TV that they both wanted to watch. It began at nine o'clock. They didn't want anything to eat. She would just stay for the show because he was feeling better now. I said, "I don't want anything to eat either, Ellen. The show is over at eleven and then you must go. Without fail." There was no reply.

At eleven the TV was still running and she had not gone, and at eleven-fifteen I went out to them. They were in bed together, her long bare arms tight around him, his face buried in her hair. I was furious and I spoke sharply.

"Ellen! This is not keeping your word to me or to your own parents! I told you distinctly that you could not stay here tonight! Now get up! Get yourself dressed! And get out of here *at once!* I'll give you no more than ten minutes!" And I turned and left them.

I was shaking with my rage. I had no compunctions about sending her home at that hour despite the distance. She had done it often, indeed just a few nights ago. But I was quite beside myself at her treachery—her whole performance—everything! There was no good in her. She had used the lowest possible appeal to the weakest in him. She had known what she was doing—had planned it. For I was remembering her words: "I like him best when he's high. Then I can get him to do what I want." I would give her ten minutes, as I had said, but no more. Not another second more.

At first there was no sound from the living room. Shortly, however, I heard a quick running and scrabbling around and then Ellen's hard heels clicking on the bare floor. She was really going. She was really going at last. And when silence fell and I heard the outer door close, I went out to speak to Gregory.

The tumbled bed was empty. Gregory had gone too.

15

*Therefore I say unto you, What things soever ye desire, when ye
pray, believe that ye receive them, and ye shall have them.*

Mark 11:24

I stood like a statue, unable to believe my eyes. Surely he hadn't
— Surely he wouldn't— Why, this was what he himself had wanted
more than anything! More, even, that he wanted Ellen! Or so I had
thought.

Ah, but he had come into my apartment in a drunken stupor. To
be sure I had—later—heard him talking. But how much had he
remembered? Ellen, though, had remembered, all right! She had
stayed clear-eyed and clearheaded while he— She *liked* him that way.
She had told me so. Ellen, I thought, with her long hungry arms.

Stunned, I moved to the tumbled bed and in an instinctive tidiness
pulled at the blanket that was half on and half off the edge. A scrap
of paper fell to the floor. I picked it up. On it were two scribbled words
in Gregory's handwriting: *"Back soon."*

But how soon was soon? And would it be soon enough? *Dear God!
Why? Oh, never mind why! Just—please—please! I know You can—*

It was half past six in the morning when I went from my bedroom
into the living room. Gregory was awake, his eyes wide and dull. The
binge at Nick's on Saturday, together with Sunday's happenings, had
taken their toll. I told him gently that I thought we had better get
started soon and he nodded and dragged himself upright. He could
hardly make his body obey his mind.

He had come in the night before about half an hour after he had
gone out with Ellen. I had been pacing restlessly with no expectation
of his appearance. When the doorbell rang and I opened to him, he

said only, with a crooked smile, "I'm back, Gram." I said I was glad, but that was all I could say. Then I asked him if he would go to bed now and he nodded. So I left him.

I don't think either of us slept at all. His radio and TV were both on through the dark hours left to us. But nothing mattered except that he had returned. Through all his muddle he had held to his resolve. Not even Ellen had been able to swerve him from it.

Fern, Gregory, and I went through the main door into the clinic of the county hospital. He had been silent the whole time it took us to get there, and Fern and I had made desultory conversation.

The waiting area was full of people, mostly boys who were there to be given their daily dose of methadone. They passed and repassed us as we went through the little gate to the desk where we were to meet Dr. Bennett. He was already there, flanked by his secretary and a nurse, with two or three figures a few steps away waiting for a word with him. He was a tall, dark-haired man with an air of impatient authority. I saw him move toward the figures as his secretary told us to find seats. He would be free presently.

"We have an appointment," I reminded her. "Dr. Bennett is to see my grandson first and give us a decision about him this morning."

I had spoken with only one thought firmly fixed in my mind. No delay. Gregory could not stand any delay. To my eyes he was on the verge of a complete collapse right then. Dr. Bennett *must* see him. Dr. Bennett *must* give us the final word of acceptance—and at once! I did not let a possible refusal enter my head. Hadn't God brought us here? *Dear God—please—please!*

We found three chairs together and sat down. The doctor was standing only a few feet away, his hands clasped behind his back, and in them I saw a letter. It was my letter, which I recognized by my handwriting. He held it crumpled open. He had received it, then. Had he had a chance to read it? I had been uncertain about writing it, but in the end I had decided to leave no stone unturned, in case Mrs. Kirk's efforts and all Gregory's records might not be enough.

It seemed a long time but actually it was only a few moments before Dr. Bennett dismissed those around him with a nod, and, turning, and without a glance in our direction, walked swiftly past us, around a corner and down a corridor where (I supposed) was his own private office. The social worker, Mr. Foster, whom Gregory had first met here and who had said he must wait six months to get admittance, was by his side.

Without any real idea of what I wanted to do except that I must keep this man in my sight, I rose and followed the two of them. I had no thought, only purpose. To save my grandson. To somehow make Dr. Bennett admit Gregory to the hospital today. *Now.* I knew I was at the last ditch. "I'll be back," I said softly to Fern. "Stay with Gregory." And there was a faint echo in my mind of his own words: *"Don't stop for anything, Gram. We've got to get there."*

I could not overtake them because of my lameness, so that the door was shut before I reached it. I looked blindly at Dr. Bennett's name on it and the word PRIVATE below that; then I raised my hand, knocked—and entered without waiting for any permission. The two men inside looked up at me in surprise. I spoke quickly, with no notion of what I was going to say.

"I am Gregory's grandmother, Dr. Bennett. I wrote you a letter telling you he has been living with me. I thought I might be able to answer some questions no one else could. That aren't in the records Mrs. Kirk sent you."

I waited, frozen at the thought of my boldness. My letter was still in his hand. He looked down at it and then at me.

"Oh, yes. Your letter. You told me about yourself. What you have been doing through the years. Writing. Very interesting."

He did not ask me to sit down but I dared to draw a breath. He had read it, then, and what I had hoped to accomplish by it, I had accomplished. For I had caught his attention. My writing had won his respect. He would, at least, give thought to what I had told him about Gregory and what I might say now.

I cannot recall with any exactness how that interview proceeded. I only remember that I remained standing throughout it all, that as we talked, Mr. Foster rose and left the room, that Dr. Bennett kept shooting questions at me, and that I replied as evenly and as intelligently as I could.

Presently he wanted to know a little more about my books, and from that he soon began talking of his own work. For he had written too. He was interested in more than psychiatry, he said. He was interested in archaeology also, and had gone on "digs" more than once with expeditions to far-off countries. In fact, he had written an article after his last journey that had appeared in the *National Geographic*. I might care to read it.

Yes, I would indeed, I said, but I was wondering how I could get the conversation back to Gregory, which was why I was there. However, he went on. He was proficient in several languages, including primitive ones, he told me, which made his archaeological trips more rewarding because he could talk to the natives. He knew not only the Romance languages but Greek, Russian, Hebrew, and Chinese. He had been to China and talked with Mao—

In desperation I broke in. "My son is a linguist too."

"No. He is not."

This flat contradiction astounded me. Until that moment he had not known I had a son. How could he say a thing like that? Suddenly I wanted to laugh. For this man—with his vast knowledge of many matters that put him at the top of the totem pole—and Gregory—in his abysmal ignorance, at the very bottom of the same pole—were alike in one respect. No one could tell either anything.

(Later, I thought I understood the reason for his seeming rudeness. If my son had been the rare kind of linguist he himself was, versed in Swahili and in other primitive tongues as well as in Mandarin Chinese, the doctor would have known him, for there were so few of them. And anyone outside of that extremely small intelligent group of people was, in his opinion, no real linguist. From that point of view I suppose he was correct.)

I quickly changed the subject. "Dr. Bennett, I'm afraid I'm taking too much of your time. It's been very good of you to give me so much. Gregory is outside your door now, waiting to talk to you. Shall I send him in?"

This was *lese majesty* indeed. But I could endure the tension no longer. I waited fearfully for his reply. He slapped his hands down on the desk.

"No. I must see another boy first. Go down to the end of my hall where you'll see a secretary by the telephone at the desk there. She will let you know when I am free."

Was this an indefinite stall? I did not know. But there was nothing more I could do except speak my thanks.

I went out. There was a boy standing there awaiting his turn, and he entered as I departed. I moved back down the corridor to where I had left Fern and Gregory.

"There's another place to sit near Dr. Bennett's office," I said. "Both of you come there with me. I don't think it will be long now." But I was not as confident as I sounded as remembrance of the enormity of my audacity swept over me.

I led them past Dr. Bennett's door to an open space where I had glimpsed a desk and a young woman before it. This was a small area where there were only a dozen or so seats. They were all empty now. We sat down and a silence fell. I threw a quick glance at Gregory. He was looking and acting like a sleepwalker, his face dead white, his eyes dark blank holes in it. How long since he had had any methadone? I had no idea. But I knew it was too long. Wouldn't Dr. Bennett see that Gregory needed immediate help? Or wouldn't he see him at all? Had I completely ruined my grandson's chances? *Please, dear God! Be with us—stay with us. Please—*

We waited. No word was spoken. Gregory sat there, his figure slumped, his head in his hands, the absolute picture of despairing, helpless hopelessness. I prayed wordlessly. Not thanks—only, repeatedly and incoherently: *Please—please—!*

The telephone tinkled. The girl at the desk picked up the receiver. Then she nodded in our direction.

"Gregory? Dr. Bennett will see you now."

Somehow Gregory got himself to his feet, and somehow he managed to propel himself in the right direction. I started to go with him but was signaled to wait. So, as he disappeared from our view, we waited. After a while—I don't know how many minutes passed but they seemed interminable—the telephone tinkled again and the secretary spoke into it and then rose to her feet.

"I'll show you two and Gregory to the admissions office now," she said.

I was alone in the large area opposite the entrance door to the clinic where we had come in earlier. I had gotten this far with Fern and Gregory and the nurse (into whose hands the doctor's secretary had put us) and we were on our way to the admissions office, when I suddenly could go no further. I was too lame and too tired. Besides, there was nothing more for me to do. I was through, my work finished. It was Fern who must fill out the necessary forms.

"I'll wait for you here, Fern," I said to her. And to Gregory, "Goodby, darling. Good luck." He did not answer or turn his head. He was just dragging himself along by sheer willpower, the nurse keeping her eyes on him as he walked. I sank down in a chair wondering if I could believe—at last—what was happening. But gradually my clouded thoughts came clear, one especially.

Gregory's life and mine together had come to an end. For he was not to return to me when he was released from the hospital. This had been settled easily and inevitably. Just as he had known, from talking with boys who had gone through the routine, what to expect there, so he had known, too, what to expect afterward.

He would have to report for his methadone every morning between seven-thirty and eight-thirty, the only hours at which the clinic was open and when the boys were treated. There were no evening hours. After telling me this he had asked if he could come back to live with me again. The answer was clear.

"Gregory," I had said, "you know I have no garage. I park my car right outside my front door. It will be January when you are free again. The dead of winter. I remember last winter we had lots of snow and ice. It used to take me a good half hour to sweep my car clean of its load of snow, to scrape off the ice on my windows, and get my motor running. I couldn't possibly guarantee to get you to the hospital so early. But if you are home again, Gregory, there are two cars there in a sheltered double garage; and if you are snowed in, there are three of you—Bruce, your dad, and you—to shovel you out. Your mom will be glad to have you home with them again, you know. They *want* you. So, isn't that best?"

Thus, easily and naturally, his sojourn with me was finished, and his reunion with his parents arranged and accepted.

Remembering all this I sat resting—until I suddenly realized Fern was taking a long time in that office. Was anything wrong at the last minute? I had to know. I pulled myself to my feet and set out to find where she was. I had to ask the way and it was a long walk, but presently I reached the right door. It was open, and within the room I saw Fern busily at work with papers on the desk before her. In front of it was the admissions officer, the telephone at her ear. Gregory was stretched out almost flat in a chair, his head back, his eyes closed, his long legs stuck straight out.

Fern saw me. Her voice was bright. "Sorry to take so long, Mother. I knew you'd get tired of waiting. But there were a lot of questions I had to answer. I'm through now, though. This is the last paper."

I heard the admissions officer speak into the phone on her shoulder. "Send Arnold. Yes. Gregory Doane. Right away, please." She turned to me and said pleasantly, "Grandmother?"

I nodded. There was another chair next to Gregory and I sat down in it. Fern was thanking the director for her cooperation when a tall young orderly wearing a blue uniform jacket appeared in the doorway.

"I'm here for Doane."

"Yes. Gregory? Gregory! Arnold is here to show you the way."

Gregory pulled himself upright. He looked at no one. He did not answer his mother's words of farewell. I offered none. Staring straight ahead, stumbling a little—swaying uncertainly but ignoring Arnold's outstretched hand, and seeing nothing—he went out the door.

The director, watching, spoke. "He's all right. He's a fighter. He'll make it."

16

I was home again. I had left Fern at her house and had just unlocked my door and entered into my disordered living room, which
I hadn't had time to tidy before leaving with Gregory early that
morning. But I scarcely noticed that as I sank down in my big blue
chair—the same chair over which I had leaned a lifetime ago when
I had surreptitiously lifted Gregory's wicked-looking knife from the
table nearby and had carried it to my bedroom to hide it in my closet.
I sat there remembering that time, when suddenly I heard myself
speaking aloud:

"I have been an instrument of the Lord."

Startled at the sound of my voice I wondered if that was really I
speaking, and if I had actually said those words. But indeed it was so.
I was unexpectedly announcing for anyone—all the world—to hear
what I had come to know was true in a surprising moment of illumina-
tion.

For in that moment I understood beyond question that my prayers,
which I had thought lost in the wild blue yonder, had indeed been
heard—and answered. Gregory was being helped, not by me but
through me. Marveling, I saw now that during all those strange and
difficult moments, there had been help for *me*—but I had been unaware. I had been upheld despite my errors and my doubts—and I had
not known. Quietly it came to me in the fallen silence that I had never
been alone—never—but always I had been guided unerringly and
unfailingly to this moment by an unrecognized Power, shown to me
in His own chosen time. Quietly I accepted it. And quietly peace

enveloped me. For God was no longer a Being, vague, mysterious, and remote. He had become a personal God who was working in my life —and who *cared*.

"Love is not enough," our minister had told us, and I had wondered what more was needed. It was then that I recalled Paul's words: "And now abideth faith, hope, charity, these three; but the greatest of these is charity" (1 Corinthians 13:13). And what is charity but love? God is love. So charity is God's love for man. Ah! There it was! *My* love for Gregory was not enough. But beyond mine there is always God's —if I had the faith to believe it. Had I? Until now it had been uncertain and wavering. But now—now— Now I knew. Now I was sure. Now I would never doubt again.

I sat there in my wing chair—thinking—remembering—*feeling* all this. And I wanted to cry. I was full of tears of joy that came trembling up from my heart. And my *Thank You, God,* was the merest whisper. But I knew He had heard. I *knew*.

There is, or should be, little else to say. Gregory, home again with his parents, a changed boy after his stay in the hospital, free of Ellen and holding down a good job— What more was to be desired?

It was he who answered that question. He wanted to be free of the need of daily methadone—free, indeed, from the need of *all* drugs. And so, by early summer, he shaped his days to that end. The decision held pitfalls, as he had been warned by his counselor, but he was confident. I myself, hospitalized at that time for hip surgery and then absorbed in my own efforts to return to an active life, was not fully aware of Gregory's progress. Thus it was over a year before I realized that my grandson, not long ago rescued and started on a new road, had slipped off it and was back in old bad habits. Once more the situation under Fern's roof was unbearable. Once more there was stormy quarreling, angry abuse, shouted defiance in a daily increasing tension. For, once more, Gregory was on drugs.

I was shaken by this knowledge and I asked over and over—*God! Why? Why did You let this happen?* But no reply came. Yet I knew, of course, God could not be blamed. Gregory had chosen, of his own free will and against advise, to give up methadone when he wasn't possessed of the strength to win the struggle this entailed.

What was to be done? He was in need of help as he had been before.

But who was to give it? Fern had already found out that the county hospital would not take him back as a patient a second time. What was the answer?

It came with a shocking suddenness when Gregory's father suffered a severe heart attack and was told by his doctor that upon his return home from intensive care he must have absolute peace and quiet for a number of weeks in order to build up his strength to endure major surgery later. When Fern told me this my reply was immediate and inevitable. "Gregory must come live with me again." For I loved Tom too. Fern, stricken to a sense of helplessness by this catastrophe in her life, was silent. I added, "My dear, why else have I recovered so wonderfully from my operation? God is telling me I am needed by Gregory again. My work with him is not ended."

She said, "Well, Mother—if you think you can—"

I had not, in my heart, really wanted to make that offer, and for two reasons. First, Gregory was involved with a girl again—Ann— and his coming to me would present sleeping problems, which I did not feel called upon to solve as I had before. But chiefly, the passage of time had separated us spiritually as well as physically, so that the rapport that had always existed between us was lessened. I knew I had his affection still, and he still gave me his courtesy whenever I saw him, but he had a new rough strength of his own and would, I felt, refuse any offer of mine. He was always ready, however, to shake off the dust of his own home, so he agreed to come—although he too felt reservations, as I did. And I was aware of this, so I was not really surprised when he appeared one day (just before his father was due to arrive home from the hospital) to present me with an alternative.

He came to tell me he had found an apartment along the river which he and Ann would like to move into. They were thinking of getting married, and they thought that living together would help them make up their minds. Between them they had enough furniture from their own rooms at home. But he hadn't sufficient money to pay the full July rent until his payday at the end of the week. He had, however, fifty dollars in cash, which would hold the place for him until Friday. He threw the bills onto my desk, asking me if I would make out a check to the landlord for that amount as he himself never had enough money to open a checking account—nor had Ann—and

he didn't want to make a cash transaction because then he would have
no record of it. If I would do this they could move in right away over
the Fourth of July holiday.

I did some quick thinking. At the time they both had well-paying
jobs which they had held all spring. And I knew they were earning
enough to swing this setup if they would just be careful with their
money. Also, I was pleased at the thought of their possible marriage.
So, as a gift, I offered Gregory a check for the entire month of July,
with the understanding that that was all I could do. They would have
to be responsible for August. I felt considerable relief over the settlement, although it was not untinged with some anxiety. However, on
the whole, it seemed the best arrangement and a happy solution for
the moment.

A moment was all it was. By the end of the month Gregory had
not saved the August rent. Nor had Ann. When they came to tell me
this, more than half believing I would come to their rescue again, I
heard their explanations about the unexpected expenses they had had
on their car (an ancient Cadillac which belonged to Ann), but I was
unmoved. "You'll just have to get out then," I said coldly. "I told you
I wouldn't do anything more. You'd better go hunt for another place.
You have only today and tomorrow to find one. If you want, I'll help
you move. Or can you afford a U-Haul?"

They didn't think so. They'd have to pay in advance for whatever
room they could find, so they would be glad if I would give them a
hand with the moving. My old Chevy would take a lot of the small
stuff. They'd start packing right away. Tonight—right after they got
home from work—they'd start.

That last night in July was terribly hot. They were both at their jobs
until five o'clock, so it was after that when I met them at their
apartment. There was another boy there who helped Gregory fill my
car. Everything that remained in their rooms after my departure they
planned to take in their big Cadillac back to Gregory's room at Fern's,
whence most of it had come. They thought they would have to make
three trips but they'd come to me as soon as they could get there to
unpack my car. What I was carrying would have to go into my place
—"temporarily."

It was long after midnight when I heard my front doorbell ring. The
superintendent's son had emptied my Chevy for me and everything

was lined up by my front door before my bookcases in an untidy mess around a mound of laundry. I opened to Gregory and Ann, who staggered in with groans of joy at my air-conditioned rooms. They were dirty, dripping, disheveled, exhausted. I brought them sandwiches I had made, some cookies, and cold drinks which they gulped down out of bottles. For a moment nothing was said. Presently I asked the question to which I already knew the answer.

"Well, what's your next stop? Where are you going from here?"

They looked at each other and then at me. Gregory gave a short laugh of surprised amusement at my words.

"Why, Gram! You know we haven't had enough time to go hunting!"

I knew. I knew very well, for it was what I had expected. So now they had no place, no plan, and no money. A flurry of angry exasperation filled me. How stupidly they lived! With never a thought for the morrow! The squirrels did better. The ants. The bees. If it weren't for Tom—but he still needed quiet and freedom from all worry before the upcoming bypass surgery he must undergo.

I said the words I had known I would say: "All right, Greg. I understand. Take Ann home to her folks and then you come back here."

They looked at each other again. Gregory gave me his radiant, confident smile. "Well, you know, Ann hates her mother, and her father hates me, so we can't go there. We were sort of hoping we could somehow stay together."

"I've told you what you can do, Greg. Take it or leave it."

He decided to take it.

It had always seemed to me that the root of Gregory's troubles lay in his inability to manage his money. What he earned was never enough, so he borrowed—or cadged off others. Or cheated. Or stole. It was the frenzied need for more than his earnings which, I believed, had driven him to selling marijuana. This, however, was always a risk and often a failure, and, not meeting with the success he had anticipated, he then turned to opiates for forgetfulness. It seemed to be a vicious circle. I thought that if he could once learn to budget, to live within his expenses, he would find and enjoy the success that was constantly eluding him, and there would be no more need for unlawful dealings or for the drinks and drugs that were ruining him.

Well, I wondered, was this my mission? Was this how God intended me to help Gregory? I decided it was.

I had several ideas. One was to force him into the habit of saving by requiring him to give me a small fixed sum each week to pay for his bed and breakfasts. I didn't need it. I would give it back to him when he left me. But it would be a good thing for him to have to do this. I thought also I would offer him and Ann the freedom of my kitchen for their meals so that they would not have to eat out all the time, for this was expensive. I was going to explain that I did not mean we would necessarily all three eat together; I was often at Fern's or out with friends. They could choose their own hours. And I would be glad to make room for their provisions on my shelves and in my Frigidaire.

I presented my suggestions the next day when they came in after their work. I began by saying I knew none of us wanted the present arrangement of living to continue indefinitely. "You two want to be together. And alone. And you should be. You can be, too. But don't you know you've got to budget? You both earn enough, but you don't handle your money right. Let me show you! Let me help you! So you can get your own little apartment somewhere soon!"

They showed small interest in the subject. With lazy laughing indolence Gregory agreed to give me five dollars a week. "Ten if you want it, Gram," he said. But the idea of eating their meals at my apartment made Ann raise an eyebrow. "We could try it. The thing is, I don't like to cook."

For my third and last idea, however, they exhibited a sudden surprising enthusiasm. That was when I offered to open a checking account in my name but in trust for Gregory, so that they might put aside something regularly every payday—whatever amount they chose—which they could see mount up. For a moment they were silent in sheer astonishment. Such a thought had never occurred to them. They'd never been able to keep open an account themselves. They had to pay too much for the service. So they had carried around with them the money they received on payday, and that was why they never had any. They didn't know where it went. It just disappeared. But to have a bank account! A place where they would know it would really be safe! It was a wonderful idea! Would I really—? How soon could I—? They could give me some right this minute! And more on Friday when they were paid! Oh, they felt rich already!

"I'll do it tomorrow," I told them.

So the next morning I went to the bank and deposited two hundred and fifty dollars—a respectable sum. And two days later, on their payday, I put in some more. Had they (I asked) saved out enough for their expenses the following week? Yes, they had. They were sure. "Don't worry, Gram." And off they went in a light and happy mood to spend the weekend somewhere—I didn't know where. They didn't tell me and I didn't ask. Gregory arrived home again about midnight Sunday.

But on Monday morning at the breakfast table he asked me to go to the bank and draw out about sixty dollars from his account. He had nothing to carry him through the week. What he'd thought was going to be enough just wasn't. They had driven down to the Island. "And you know that takes a lot of gas. Then there was the motel too. Anyway, it's all gone. Better make it a hundred, just to be on the safe side," he finished with a bright and easy confidence.

I looked at him unbelievingly. "Really, Greg," I said, after a minute, "there's not going to be much point in this if you take money out as fast as you put it in."

He was suddenly truculent. "It's my money!"

My surprise held me silent. He had never spoken in such a tone to me before. I looked into his eyes and had a swift understanding. Drugs. He'd been on them over the weekend. Some was left in his system. That was what made him speak to me in such a rude way. And that was where his money had gone. He got up from the table and, over his shoulder as he went to the door, he said, "I'll be home in my noon hour to get it."

He had given me an order. When he was high he could be lordly. Anyway, I went to the bank and when he appeared at noontime I handed it over to him without a word. He did not thank me.

Around six o'clock that day the two of them appeared together from work. They acted constrained. I waited for them to speak, and it was Gregory who broke the awkwardness, his manner defying me to interrupt or interfere.

They wanted to tell me, they said, that they did not, after all, like the idea of a trust account with me being the only person who could draw out their money. They had decided they would prefer to have a joint account against which they could both draw. Then they could handle their own affairs and there would never be any question about anything. It would be much better.

"I agree," I said quietly. "Shall we go up to the bank right now? It's Monday night, so it's open."

Yes. They would like that. We went, I in their car with them. On the way we were all very polite to each other. At the bank I introduced them to the president, explained what they wanted to do and then withdrew to the lobby to wait for them. When they emerged we got into their car again, and, still all very polite, we drove home.

"We're going out for dinner tonight, Gram," Gregory said, as they waited for me to get out of their car at the front steps of the apartment. "I don't know how long we'll be out. Or when we'll be back. We have some business to take care of."

Their business! Buying and selling marijuana. I nodded and they drove away. I unlocked my door and went in past all Ann's stuff, which was still piled before my bookcases, including the great mound of unwashed laundry. I should have known it would end this way. And I was disgusted with them. Children! That was all they were. Responding to the whim of the moment. They did not *want* to have their own apartment. Not really. They did not *want* to budget and get in the clear financially. What did they want? Did they know themselves? They were chasing a pot of gold at the foot of a marijuana rainbow. They were going down a blind alley to a dead end.

And—perhaps—so was I!

17

*Rest in the Lord, and wait patiently for him: fret not thyself
because . . . of the man who bringeth wicked devices. . . .*

Psalms 37:7

It is difficult to write of the remainder of that month with Gregory.
Briefly—it was a nightmare. The bank incident had estranged us and
one thing after another increased this estrangement until finally we
were living in a marked suspicion and mistrust. What I prayed for
during that interval was strength to maintain my self-control.

I did not like Ann. She had a soft, ingratiatingly innocent way of
imposing on me. Within three days Gregory's closet was filled with
her pantsuits, her bright-colored high-heeled shoes, her lotions and
creams and powders and perfumes as well as her hair dryer, her
makeup box, and her hand mirror. Except for sleeping she practically
lived with us and was always showering, tinting her nails, washing her
hair, or changing her clothes to go out with Gregory. She would say,
"You don't mind, do you?"

But I did mind. Wet towels left on the bathroom floor, long hair
in the kitchen sink, empty bottles left anywhere— Besides, I did not
trust her. Her glance would fix itself dreamily on something I was
wearing—a pin, a ring, a necklace—so that I very shortly decided to
empty my jewel box and keep its contents in unlikely places such as
my shoe bag or the carton of Christmas decorations on my closet
shelf, which had hidden things before.

I did not trust Gregory either. I had to conceal from him my small
supply of sleeping pills and my painkilling drugs. (My right hip was
giving me trouble, as my left one had earlier.) It seemed best to keep
all these in my handbag, which I carried on my arm from room to
room, even to the telephone and into the bathroom. In my bag also

were credit cards, my driver's license, and my keys, including the one for my car. Gregory had asked for a key to the apartment for himself so that he could come in at any time he wanted, but I was not going to have him and Ann in my place when I was not there.

It was a horrid way to live.

Gregory, who was on probation for several misdemeanors, was supposed to meet with his probation officer once a week and give to him some payment, however small, toward the settlement of his debt to the state. But he did not go often and he had reduced his debt very little. Finally his probation officer telephoned Fern, unaware that Gregory was not living at his own home, and told her that her son would be arrested if he did not appear that very day to report his activities and hand over some money. Fern relayed this message to me and I relayed it to Gregory, who at once flew into a rage, using language shocking to me as he had never done in my presence before. I waited for him to stop before I spoke.

"Gregory, you don't make sense. You know perfectly well you don't want to be arrested and go to jail. Who do you think would bail you out? I certainly won't. And your father can't be troubled by such things now. Listen. Ann isn't here and you don't know when she will be, so come in my car with me. I will take you to your probation officer. And I will lend you a few dollars to give him."

This enraged him again. It was all none of my business! Why was I suddenly hassling him? He would wait for Ann. She had only gone for gas. She would be back in a few minutes and then *she* would take him. Yes, he'd go all right. But he wouldn't give one cent to that guy. Not one red cent! He didn't have any to spare. In fact, he didn't have any at all.

He always had it for their car. For meals out. For whatever he and Ann wanted. Or indeed for what he alone wanted. But he never had any for payment to anybody else. Not once had he given me the five dollars he had so glibly and grandly agreed to give me. There had always been some excuse or reason why he didn't have it at the moment, so I soon dropped the matter. Nor was there ever any offering of help to me in lieu of this. No carrying of trash to the cellar, no mopping of the kitchen floor, no washing of any windows. And their mound of soiled laundry was still before my bookcases although

I had repeatedly asked them to remove it. Everything else was still there too.

By now their manner was that they were doing me a favor by giving me their company. It was a ridiculous idea on my part, I kept telling myself. Incredible. But that was how I felt. They came and went with an airy, sometimes total, disregard of my presence, often not speaking to me at all, any more than to the furniture in the room. I might have been a chimera, and I began to feel I was being ostracized in my own home. But I endured all this because I knew words would change nothing but only make matters worse. With sorrow I realized that whatever rapport I had once had with Gregory was now completely gone. At least, however, I was keeping Fern and Tom untroubled— and my own emotions leashed.

There was, I knew, a growing hatred toward me in their hearts because of a situation they did not like and could not alter until their underground activities prospered. I myself felt no hatred. Only an increasing sickness of soul because so much of time, effort, hope, and belief had gone down the drain. Why? I kept asking. *Why,* dear God? Why everything for nothing?

Nothing. Yes. I admitted it at last, and my earlier faith was shaken. As an instrument of the Lord, I was a failure this time. Was this my fault? Where had I gone wrong? I did not know, and my confidence diminished when I received no answer. Once again God became a distant figure to me, one no longer concerned with me in my life.

And how much longer could I bear living this way? Inevitably, I knew, there must come an end.

Gregory, charming when he wanted to be, good-looking, quick-witted, willing, and seemingly competent, had always been able to get jobs, but he was invariably so casual about them that he often lost them in a short time. The one he was holding down at present he liked because it paid well and the hours he worked were the same as Ann's. He would drive her to her office first, then, in her car, drive to his factory across town. His immediate superior was easygoing and seemed not to mind when Gregory took time off without first seeking permission. But there came a day when he did this once too often. Cashing his paycheck, which was always given at noon on Friday, he and a fellow worker failed to report back. Ann, who had been brought

to my apartment at the end of the day by a friend when Gregory had
not come for her, was first angry and then worried as he did not
appear. But when she finally opened my door to him at seven o'clock,
her anger vanished before her relief. I, having had my supper, had
retreated to my room, leaving my door open and so heard Ann's quick
question and his reply.

"Where in the world have you been?"

"Upstate!" His tone was jubilant.

"How come?"

"Went to see an artist Jim knew about who does tattoos. I wanted
one. Look at my arm! Isn't that a beautiful devil?" And he laughed.

She laughed, too. "I'll say! How much did that cost?"

"Twenty bucks."

Hearing this, I quietly closed my door, then I spoke softly aloud.
"Dear God, give me strength to keep my silence. Give me strength!
Please!"

They were gone over that weekend again. The following Monday
after Gregory had left for his job I was surprised to see him drive up
to my door within an hour later. Jim was with him and they came in
laughing.

"We were fired," Gregory said cheerfully. "It wasn't my boss. *He*
didn't care about Friday. It was the chief. I didn't like that work
anyway. It was smelly—mixing up all those chemicals for their deter-
gents. And there was no air conditioning up under the roof where the
tanks are. Don't worry, though, Gram. I've already got a lead to
something else. Jim told me about it."

I nodded and left them alone, still laughing together. Presently they
both departed and Gregory did not come back until he brought Ann
at five o'clock. They went immediately into the kitchen and I heard
them at the telephone. I approached the doorway to ask if they were
making an out-of-town call, for that was the one thing I was adamant
about. They must pay for those. Seeing me, Gregory drew me into the
living room, for Ann was doing the talking.

"Yes, it's long distance," he told me. "But it's a poor connection
so we'd better stay here. Well, I'll tell you. She's trying to get a
reservation for us up north a ways for this coming weekend. We're
tired of Long Island. She's been to this place and she says it's great.

We can rent a horse and ride all day if we want. Sounds good, doesn't it!"

As if he had not just lost his job. As if he owed nobody anything. As if money grew on trees. Twenty dollars for a tattoo. And now a weekend of horseback riding at some ranch a hundred or more miles from here. And never a cent for me. A sudden fury boiled up in me. And it wasn't just because he was paying me nothing. It was for the whole ramshackle mess he was making of his life. Abruptly, I couldn't bear it any longer. Or him. Or Ann. Or anything. I gave him one look and then, without a word, I went through my front door with my handbag over my arm and got into my car, which was parked in the driveway there. I had to leave them both alone there for a little while, whether they helped themselves to anything of mine or not.

I was gone about an hour. When I went back to my apartment Ann and Gregory were, to my surprise, still there, sitting on the sofa bed holding hands. I did not ask if they had secured their reservations. I did not speak a word. I simply went past them carrying somewhat awkwardly the five sizable cartons I had picked up and had wedged together so I had two in one hand and three in the other. I bore these past their astonished and curious eyes to my bedroom. Then I joined them and sat down in my wing chair.

"You are wondering about those cartons. Well, I'll explain. They are for Ann's clothes and other things that she has parked in your closet, Gregory. I will either call the Salvation Army to come get these cartons full of Ann's things or I will ask the superintendent to carry all five to the trash room in the cellar, which is cleared out every single morning. Without any further word to you than this warning I am giving you now, that will happen." I paused. All this had been said in a quiet, perfectly controlled voice. I finished in the same way. "In ten days there will be a Labor Day weekend holiday. You may stay here until Labor Day. No longer. That will be the end." And I rose and went back to my room.

They had not spoken. Some time later they went out very quietly, and then I telephoned Fern to tell her of my ultimatum. "I know you wanted me to keep Gregory here until his court case comes up about breaking probation, but we don't know when that will be. And I've had it, Fern. I've *had* it." She said, "I understand, Mother."

Through the next few days there was a hushed, almost sepulchral
silence in my apartment whenever they came into it. Actually they
were there very little. I did not know if they had secured the reservations they had wanted or not. I did not care. We kept an armed truce.
When Friday came, they rushed in, grabbed up a few things, and
rushed out again. They did not say where they were going and of
course I did not ask. I just hoped they would remember I had said,
"—*until* Labor Day."

Friday night—all day Saturday—Saturday night—and all day Sunday—and I had heard nothing from them. I hoped they were hunting
for another place to stay but I could not guess. They could be fritter-
ing away their time and money as usual. It would not surprise me.
And at the thought anger boiled up in me once again, though I tried
to stay calm. At midnight I went to bed but I could not sleep. Finally
I got up, my anger now cold in my heart, and dragged those five
cartons from my bedroom to the closet that was Gregory's in the
dinette. For the next couple of hours I was busy packing every last
thing that belonged to Ann. I did it carefully so powder wouldn't spill
or bottles break. I was even careful about the creases in Ann's pantsuits. But at last I had put in the last thing. Then I showered and went
to bed. But still I did not sleep. Was this a dreadful thing I was doing?
I did not feel it was. I did not feel anything. I had warned them. I had
said, "—*until* Labor Day." And this was Labor Day.

In the morning at about nine o'clock I telephoned Ann's mother.
I told her that Gregory was not going to be with me any longer, and
as many of Ann's clothes were here in his closet, I thought they had
better be picked up and taken to her own home. Since it was a holiday,
probably her husband was available to come get them. I would wait
for him to appear until ten-thirty. If he was not here by then, I would
conclude they did not want to bother and I would dispose of them as
I saw fit.

"Where is she now?" Ann's mother demanded. And I replied that
I had no idea. Then I hung up.

At ten o'clock my doorbell sounded. A short gray-headed man
stood there whom I had never seen before. "I've come for my daughter's clothes," he said.

I nodded as I opened the door wide. "She has a lot of other stuff
here too," I told him, and I indicated the collection still piled up

before my bookcases. "Please take everything."

He did. Without another word to me he began grimly carrying out all her possessions to his station wagon. Then he drove away.

It was late that Sunday afternoon when Gregory and Ann finally put in an appearance. I was resting on my sofa. They did not greet me as I looked up. (I had purposely left the door open for them.) I might have been a wax figure lying there. I did not speak either. I watched Ann go straight to the closet in the adjoining dinette to pick out a change of clothes for herself. She apparently had not noticed the empty area before the bookcases. Gregory had dropped wearily into a chair, not looking at me at all, though I saw his glance go toward the bookcases without either curiosity or surprise. He seemed sunk in fatigue. Then I looked again at Ann, who had opened the two folding doors of the closet and now turned to me in slow astonishment and disbelief.

"Where are my things?"

"Your father came for them this morning. They're all now at your house, I imagine. He took everything." Then I added, "I warned you."

She said nothing. Gregory said nothing. Then, seeing his clothes still hanging there, she rushed to a small chest, yanked open a drawer, and pulled out a clean pillowcase of mine. Into this she swept all that was there of Gregory's, including his dirty high boots. "I'll take Greg's things!" she exclaimed.

I made no reply. I waited. The only words Gregory spoke were addressed to Ann. "We'll have to go to your house now first. Then we'll go to New York."

New York. Had they found a room there then? I wondered but I did not ask and I was not told. The silence was heavy. I watched him slowly rise, walk toward the door, which Ann had reached first, and take the stuffed pillowcase from her. Then, without a backward glance or another word, they went away. I shall never forget.

I was alone. I was empty. Drained. It was the second time Gregory had done this to me. But it was the last. For this time I was free of him. I felt no anger, no bitterness, no regret. Nothing. Simply—I was free. Once I read that as you grow older your responses to emotional situations atrophied until finally nothing much mattered anymore. At long last, I thought, this is happening to me.

But I could at least be glad that Tom was still alive and well. Well enough to face the necessary surgery, through which ordeal he came most successfully. It was while he was in St. Luke's that I entered the Presbyterian Hospital for my second hip operation. We were both home again by Christmas, both without pain and both definitely on the mend. For both of us I sent up heartfelt prayers of thanks.

I had much to be thankful for besides my return to health. I had a devoted family and I had three more grandsons (two were my son's), in whom I took much pride. But aside from my prayers of thankfulness I asked God for nothing. Nothing more in the way of help from Him for Gregory was needed, for I was not dealing with him any longer. He was out of my life.

And, indeed, he had removed himself geographically as well by now because, finding New York too expensive as well as too dangerous for drug transactions, he had taken himself to Florida again—once again breaking probation, as he went without getting permission first. Ann refused to go with him. Upon his arrival he telephoned back to Fern to let her know he was all right. (And I thought, with remote interest, how strange it was that he never wholly lost touch with his family.) But when she went on to say that he had given her his address and did I want it, my answer was quick and decisive.

"No. I am not going to write to him."

I was, then, quite through with Gregory, and I could not care less. Gregory had used me and abused me. That was all there was to it. Sometimes through the days that followed I felt as if I were living in a curious vacuum, as if I were waiting for something, although I didn't know even remotely what it might be. Perhaps, I thought, it was a kind of trusting. I wasn't sure. Anyway, it seemed to be all that was left of my faith that had once been so strong in my heart. If God had ever answered my question—*Why?* But He hadn't.

And then another question came to my mind. Where was it I had read—"Trust in the Lord with all thine heart; and lean not unto thine own understanding"? (Proverbs 3:5.) Ah! Hadn't I always leaned too much on my own understanding? When God was *there*. Always there —*somewhere*. This I had been brought up to believe. He was there somewhere—waiting. And so I waited too.

18

If it was difficult to write the preceding chapter, it is still more
difficult to write this one. For who will believe it? Who in the world
will believe it?

It was now six months since Gregory had gone south. Six months
since I had said I would not write to him. Six months—and I had not
heard from him either, though I hadn't really expected or wanted to.

And then, sometime in June, the postman pushed through my mail
slot a letter from my grandson. He wrote as though no enmity had
ever existed between us, as though the past were wiped out. "I'm sorry
I haven't written you sooner" was his beginning. (And why was he
writing me now, I wondered?) He wanted to tell me that he planned
to marry a girl named Kay. "She is a beautiful person." But they
couldn't do that until he got out of jail. He would be in for several
months but the charges against him were not too serious. They just
meant a lot of time. "So don't worry." (A familiar phrase, that.) He
might (he went on) be transferred later back to this state for having
left here without permission. If that happened Kay would come and
they would be married in prison. It was allowed. "I'm glad this has
happened, Gram, because after this I'll have nothing hanging over me.
I have some money. I miss everybody, especially you." And, surpris-
ingly, he ended by saying—"I'm doing some reading in a psychology
book and trying to understand myself and other people better. Please
write me if you feel like it. Love, Greg."

I read this unexpected letter without any emotion, but his last sentence stirred my curiosity. It was unlike him to be reading a book on psychology! Could it be true? If so, where had he gotten it? I called Fern, who had heard from him several times. She was glad he had finally written me. No, he had not mentioned any such book to her. Did I think I would reply to him? I said I would because I wanted to find out about that psychology book.

He answered my query at once. He was glad to hear from me. He hoped my hip wasn't bothering me anymore. He had gotten the book from the jail library. There was air conditioning in the jail too. It was the best jail in Florida, if you must be in one. He finished by saying —"I'm not mad at being here, Gram. I'm actually happy. I can't explain it but I feel different."

He wrote Fern too in somewhat the same vein, and we compared our letters. Against all reason and memory our feeling grew slowly that some transformation was taking place in Gregory. Perhaps because of this Kay. Or perhaps because, for the first time, a long confinement was giving him time to think—to review his past and look ahead to his future. We didn't know and could only hope. But definitely some change was going on, because in almost every letter —and I was receiving two or three a week—there would be the refrain "I've changed quite a bit . . . I feel different about a lot of things. . . . I can't explain. It's mostly a feeling I have." We read these revelations and wondered. However, we could not wholly trust or believe what we read. And Tom was wholly skeptical.

Still the letters kept coming. And I continued to answer. I had become increasingly intrigued. Some of his sentences, dropped anywhere on his one brief page, were really incredible. "I do truly believe I've reached a turning point." And—"It's come to me that I want to change my life. My whole way of life. . . . I've got a goal now and it's something I want. . . . I want to start fresh." And, over and over, "I've changed a lot, Gram. You'll see. I'm glad this will be ended in a few more months."

I asked myself if Gregory was astute enough to plan a campaign such as this, believing he would be returned to his home state and so paving the way for a warm reunion with us together with complete forgiveness? My uncertainty made me measure out my words with care.

"I do want very much to see you again, Greg. I am looking forward to it and to discovering for myself all these changes in you that you say have transformed your thinking. I hope we can have some good talks. But I also want to make one thing quite clear. I am no longer able or willing to have you stay with me. I have grown accustomed to silence and solitude and know I must have them." Then, lest this seem unkind, I went on, "I wake up early in the morning, Gregory, around four o'clock, and often don't sleep again for thinking about you and your future. What is it to hold? I do wonder. And somehow that question reminds me of your last letter to me and your query in it. You wanted to know if I was still writing that book I told you I was, all about you. You asked if I had finished it yet. I was surprised that you remembered it at all. Well, yes—I finished it. But the publisher didn't like the ending. I stopped where you came home from the hospital—cured. He felt I had left you 'in limbo,' was the way he put it. He wanted some positive assurance that you were firmly established in a new and better life. And of course I couldn't give him that because you *weren't*. It's got to be true, you know, like the rest of it. So I'm stuck."

Fern was steadier than I in her reactions to Gregory's letters. She was sure of his conversion. I was a little envious of her certainty because I had felt deserted by God, while her confidence in Him, His wisdom and His Power, were unshaken. She had, for many years, been actively interested in a prayer group, finding in its membership strong spiritual support and an understanding love. Several times she asked me if I would like to join them, but I have always been a private person and I did not think I could comfortably (or, indeed, at all) share my most intimate thoughts and feelings with people I scarcely knew. I also felt I would be on a lower, less knowledgeable level which would perhaps make communication still more difficult. However, I always listened to anything she wanted to tell me. And indeed it was she who said to me during my last travail with Gregory, "Mother, you know there's nothing in the Bible that tells us God will spare us pain."

I think I must say here that I no longer went with any regularity to my own church because of the effort involved in getting there and also because of my difficulty in hearing the minister. So, instead, I turned on my television and tried the various offerings there. The most popular one seemed to be selling religion Hollywood style, with a great show of stunning sets and the introduction of important visitors; but however beautiful the presentation, I was somehow offended. What I wanted was a program that was simple, sincere, and believable. I found it quite by chance one Sunday morning early in July.

When I tuned in, a chorus of young people was singing the opening hymn, moving about the stage with an easy, careless grace that was almost a dance as their voices joyously filled the air. They were very natural, not at all like a paid group of singers standing stiffly and looking pious. They were singing because they wanted to sing, because they loved being there and doing what they were doing. As I watched their radiant smiling faces, I felt my heart lift in a glad silent response. At their finish, the minister, advancing from the wings with a buoyant, eager step, came to the front of the stage, and, descending the steps, seated himself informally on its edge, looked directly at me, lifted his hand, and, pointing a finger at me too, said in his deep, rich, warm voice, "Something *good* is going to happen to you."

I was startled by the impression I had that he was personally addressing me, but at the same time—so positive, so certain, so calmly confident was he of his words—that I found myself accepting and believing them. For no reason at all I believed what he had said, and quite unaccountably I knew a swift and leaping joy. I cannot describe how it permeated my whole being so that I felt transformed in some curious way. It made the half hour that followed strange and beautiful as I listened to the man before me saying— What was he saying? Simple things. Familiar things. But he spoke them with such candor, such conviction, and such sincerity that they became true for me in a new and sudden sharpness. "You must forgive your enemies. You must forgive all those who hurt you. The Bible says 'For if ye forgive not men their trespasses, neither will your Father forgive yours.'" (*See* Matthew 6:15.) And I thought—He is telling me I must forgive Gregory.

He went on in his quiet forceful way. "What you must never forget is that God cares about you. He never stops caring. He is in the midst of your life with all its problems all the time. Because He cares. Because God is love." And I thought—God is love—yes. I know that. He still cares about Gregory even if I don't. But if I can forgive him —and now I have—then I must love him too. Not with my love, but with the love that God has given me; yes, I can love Gregory with *God's* love—and I can forgive him, because God has forgiven me. Love and forgiveness: God has given me both, and I must give both to Gregory.

And, finally—"Let God's way be your way, for all He does works together for good." Well, there it was again, I thought. Let God's way —which I neither know nor understand—be my way. Let God's way be my way. Would I never learn?

It was over. He had finished—and I—who had been uplifted and upheld through every word he had spoken, absorbed as I had never been before by any minister— I knew that a change had taken place in me.

How can I tell it? Simply—I was alive again. I was born again. Everything felt new. The bleakness in which my spirit had been wrapped so long, was gone. Once more I hoped. Once more I loved —yes, even Gregory—and once more I believed. Only this time I understood it was more than the flash of a single bright moment as when I had discovered I was God's instrument. This time I knew I had entered into a wholly new life of growth and a new way of living that was not yet clear to me.

I was still in the grip of an emotion when that young chorus, moving with the same lovely grace, raised their voices in the last hymn. "Greater is He that is in your heart than he that is in the world." What were they saying? Simply—God is greater than any evil force in the world. They knew it. And in that instant I knew it, too. And my thoughts flew to Gregory. When would *he* know it? When?

I wanted to write to Gregory of the experience with Christ I had had which had so strangely and strongly affected me, for it was my hope that if Gregory would only tune in just once, he too might be helped in whatever metamorphosis he was going through. It was only a hope, but I knew he would enjoy the music anyway.

So I ventured, beginning first to tell about the chorus:

> You won't hear any long solemn hymns, Greg. You'll hear a jubila-
> tion and you'll see a dance. You'll like to watch and listen, for these
> are all young people. Then, when the minister comes on—well, you'll
> like him, too, I'm sure. I know you aren't interested in church affairs,

Greg, but this program is so *different!* As the minister is too. Oh, I don't know how to tell you!

Well, I'll try. Listen. The minister doesn't talk about *religion* at all. What he talks about is *living.* And how to make it better for yourself by asking God to help you in it—because God *cares.* Somehow he makes God seem a *person,* Greg. A friend who is standing by. Someone you can count on because He *cares* and knows everything you are doing and wants to help you—if you'll let Him. I'm telling you about him—this minister—because I want to ask you to listen to him at least *once.* Surely you have a TV in your jail if you have a library!

I'm afraid I haven't said all this very well. I guess I'm like you, who wrote me—"It's more a feeling I have." Well, with me this is much more than a feeling. I'm a new person. As you were trying to be, Gregory. Jesus met me right where I was, and helped me. I believe He can help you too. So listen to this man speak of Jesus, the living Jesus—just once, won't you please, darling? And write me how you like him.

His reply was prompt and angry and emphatic:

Gram! Please don't write me any more about religion! It's been shoved at me all my life. You never did this before! And I don't want it. Do don't do it again. I don't believe in it. I don't like it. I think what I want to think—and it's *not* about God. So no more. Please!

Love, Greg

My reply to him was equally prompt:

All right, Greg. Nothing more about religion. To me, though, that word simply means what you live by. And before we leave this subject I want to tell you what mine is. I can say it in one word—*Love.*

And to me love is just giving, forgiving, and helping. That was my religion, and it's what brought you to live with me twice.

But—and please read this part carefully because it's the last time I shall mention it—our life together didn't work out, and I have just realized why. My love wasn't enough, because I hadn't asked God to help me with you. I tried to use just my own strength. Now, since that sermon I listened to, I know I should have let Him in to run our life together His way.

But there's just one more thing I must say now before I ring down the curtain. It's about *your* religion. For you have one, you know. It's what *you* live by. And it is to get money. That's all. Never mind how. Just get it. And keep it. For yourself. For what *you* want. That's your religion, Gregory. What do you think of it? Are you proud of it? I ask you to think about yours. And mine. Just think about them. And now no more.

Love, Gram

I quote verbatim his incoherent, excited, emotional, and most revealing response to that. It took my breath away by its complete unexpectedness and its force. And while I was sure some words and expressions had been lifted from his psychology book—what did it matter? He knew what they meant, for behind them lay a strange wild tumultuous triumph:

My dearest, beloved Gram! I love you! I do! Upon receiving your letters I am filled with joy. I hope these feelings find you in the same way. . . . I write you because you know better than anyone where I'm at. You have unveiled the covering of my selfishness—and that is *good,* Gram. That is very good. I strive now to be flexible in my convictions as I now look into my future, which I do not want to jeopardize. I ask for your forgiveness as I know I have it. . . . I see many things now in a different perspective. . . . To tell you would take a short life to explain. Write all you want to about that minister.

Love, Greg

P.S. I'm going to give you a good ending for your book.

In a quiet wonder I read that again and again. I closed my eyes and sent heavenward the most fervent thanks I had ever offered. Then I called Fern.

Could we believe what this seemed to be saying? And promising? Did we dare? Yet how could we *not* dare?

It was September. The long hot summer had crept by. Fern talked with her minister and read him parts of Gregory's letters. He said— "Give him more time." I conferred with my publisher who said, "Wait awhile."

Wait. Wait for God's time. Not one of our choosing.

And then Gregory wrote:

> Did I tell you? I finally signed the extradition papers. Now the state can come get me. I wanted to do this. I want to clear my record. When I do get clear finally, Kay and I will get married and go west. But I'll see y'all first.

> Love, Greg.

On September 11 Fern received the following letter:

> Hillsborough Jail, Florida
> September 9, 1975

> Hi y'all! Hope everything is fine. Well, here I am and here it is Tuesday and I haven't heard another word about the state as of yet. I'm gonna tell y'all right now, Mom and Dad, that I'm sorry for all that I've put you through. I know we don't get along and you've lost faith in me as your eldest son. I don't blame you one damn bit. You haven't come out and said as much but I can tell all too well. So if I come back from Florida here and do turn up there, I won't stay with you. Okay? I hope y'all are doin' good. I hope Bruce keeps y'all together for I haven't. As I said before I'm sorry I'm a disappointment to the family as of so far. I'll try my hardest to get straight so y'all can be proud. But my words are nothing until I prove myself to you.

> Love, Greg

Was this an admission? A confession? A new beginning? It could be all three. Oh, something *good* had indeed happened to me!

Thank You, God! Thank You! And now please stay with Gregory. Help him. For he will need help. Speak to him! Speak to his heart! Please, God! *Please!*

19

As the heavens are higher than the earth, so are my ways higher than your ways, and my thoughts than your thoughts.

Isaiah 55:9

Gregory was brought back to the county jail in this state after sending us his letter of admission and contrition. Fern and I went to see him immediately. It was plain that his mood was jubilant, though the talking—the shouting, rather—was difficult through the perforated metal box that acted both as receiver and transmitter of the primitive telephone affixed solidly against the opaque yellowed-glass window between us. Even so, we gathered that he did not need money. He had enough to engage a lawyer, whom he had already seen once briefly. And he expected to go with this lawyer before a judge the following week to find out what his future would be concerning his release.

"Don't worry!" He told us. "This is going to work out. The lawyer thinks he can help shorten my sentence." He was well aware that he was charged with more than just breaking probation for going to Florida without permission. His very first offense years earlier had been for "possession of marijuana with intent to sell," which calls for a five-year imprisonment. And this charge preempts all others.

He was released on bail the following week. True to his decision not to live at home, he had made plans to stay with various friends and did not appear at Fern's except for brief visits—to get a shower, clean clothes, a meal, or to make contact with some one he knew. This arrangement seemed to suit everyone. Often he took into Fern's kitchen with him some of his companions. A few she remembered but many were new to her. One day when I was there he said, "Those two men who have just left here are the ones who are shadowing me."

"What do you mean, Gregory?" Fern asked in quick alarm. "Who are they? And why are they following you?"

"They don't trust me. I'm still on probation, you know. They have my record. They're narcs. On the narcotic squad. They've been assigned to keep an eye on me. They know I've said I want to clear my record, but they don't believe that or trust me at all. They think I'm still dealing and they want to find out who are the people I see. They want me to be useful to them. Help them spread a net. So—though I seem to be free, I'm not."

I spoke bluntly. "Well, *are* you dealing, Gregory?"

"Gram! *No!* Not anymore. They want me to. They're offering me inducements to play in with them. But I'm through with trouble. I'm here to wipe the slate clean."

He pleased me. His manner, his looks, his straightforward simple words all pleased me. Yes, he had indeed "changed quite a bit." It was evident that he was no longer on drugs and hadn't been for some time. For he was clear-eyed and poised and calm and bore himself with dignity and thoughtfulness.

A few days later I encountered this thoughtfulness when he asked me to drive him a few miles to Cliff Park, where he was staying. It was the first time I had been alone with him, and as we started on our way I waited for him to speak first. I felt that the bubbling confidence which had been his in the jail had settled into something quite different. He was grave and absorbed in his thoughts, and I wondered if he was discovering that getting his record clear was not going to be as simple as he had anticipated. When he spoke finally it was to say that the officer who had brought him north—Jim—and who seemed to be in charge of the narcs on his trail, had told him he was quite sure that the five-year sentence would be commuted to only one. "But it's going to be tricky to work out," he said.

He fell silent again after that, and I waited while I tried to guess what he was thinking about as he looked down the long road ahead of him. Suddenly he said—"Gram?"

"Yes, Gregory?"

"Are you still writing that book about me?"

Once more I was surprised at his question, but I answered as I had before. "I can't, Gregory. I'm stuck. I thought I told you. I can't write anything more until I get a new, different ending for it. A *good* ending.

When I get that I'll finish the story. But only you can give it to me."

For a long moment he was quiet. Then—"I'll *give* you a good ending, Gram. I'll *give* it to you! I told you once in a letter I would, didn't I? And you'll *like* it," he finished, with a defiant firmness in his voice.

I said softly, "I'll be terribly glad, Greg. But tell me! How long must I wait for this good ending—the ending I will like? Till you are really free? Or can it be sooner?"

He was silent once more. Finally—carefully—he gave me an answer. "Maybe—in a few more weeks—" Pause. "—if things work out." Pause. "I'm not sure yet, but maybe—" Pause. And then, with a long, slow breath— "I hope!" He stopped.

I felt he was having problems so I spoke carefully. "Do you want to talk about it more than that, Gregory?"

"I'd—rather not."

"All right, darling."

I left him where he had asked to be dropped. He thanked me. I went home, reassured that his resolution was still firm and hard. But it was curious, I thought, how he seemed to be concerned about my finishing that book I had been writing about him. It mattered to him. It had taken on a great and imperative importance to him, and this was somewhat puzzling until—suddenly—I understood why.

Gregory was hungry for success as he had always been and for the adulation that goes with it. Bruce had known both, but Gregory had been meted out scoldings and punishments through which he lost sight of the love that lay behind these things. In rebellion, anger, and jealousy—and to make a name for himself—he had taken a wrong turning years ago. But the success he had won in his illegal drug dealings had brought him no sense of triumph after all. For his parents, with whom he had always kept in touch, and to whom he invariably returned, did not give him the reward of their pleasure in him. They still censured him. They were still disapproving and disappointed. They were not proud of him or anything he did.

So his own self-pride began to dwindle. His tricks, skill in evading capture, cunning, courage, and daring—even the applause of his peers —began to lose their allure and their value. He had not increased his stature at home as, with persistent hope, he had expected. Even the financial independence he had won, which would now free him from his old life, had not brought him their respect. So it was not enough. What he wanted now, therefore, above everything, was to stand tall with them at last. To stand tall not only in their eyes but in his own —and in the eyes of the world too. To stand tall without fear or favor. It was a human need.

This was now quite clear to me. And more. Because the "good ending" he would give me for my book—if he took his punishment and cleared his record—would, in one lightning moment accomplish all this. In a single lightning moment it would bring him a praiseworthy success about which not only his family but everyone he knew —perhaps indeed the whole country—would hear. Oh, yes! I understood that was in his mind! This grandson of mine *ached* to be good, but he ached also for the adulation won—and deserved—because he would have *proved* he was good. And this, too, was a human need.

There was, I knew, almost a desperation in this longing of Gregory's to be accepted fully by his own kind. But humans have another need too, and that is to know they are accepted by God.

And when would Gregory realize this?

It was Thursday morning, the day Fern and I did our weekly shopping together. When I went for her in my car and she joined me she said, in a low voice, "Pray, Mother. Pray as you've never prayed before."

"Why? What has happened?"

"I'll tell you when we park at the shopping center." And she did.

Gregory had returned home to them last evening and had asked if he might stay all night there. He had a "hard decision" to make, he said, and he wanted to talk it over with them.

Briefly—he had to let Jim know if he, Gregory, was ready and willing to join forces with him and his squad to help them in their war against drug dealers. After watching him for days they had liked what they found and had believed in his sincerity about wanting to clear his record. So the moment had come for him to prove this by throwing in with them. Either that—or take his punishment. "Five years, Mother," he had reminded her. "Or—if I do this—maybe only one." But he must decide at once. Tonight. Tonight he had to set up a situation, introduce them to some one of his so-called helpers—one of his "friends"—and put through a sale of a desired narcotic. Heroin.

"Or else—" he had finished. And stopped. She stopped, too.

I sat in silence, stunned and dumbstruck. After a moment I asked her what advice she had given, what she had said.

"I told him," she replied, "that we couldn't make that decision for him. Or give him any advice. It was his life. He had chosen it. He would have to make up his own mind and choose which way he was going now." She paused. "Then I asked him if he had thought what this could mean. To all of us." She shook her head. "He hadn't. He knew he was putting his own life on the line. But he hadn't thought about Bruce. Bruce is just the same height as he is, I reminded him, and wears his hair long the same way, in a ponytail on his neck, and they're both bearded and about the same coloring. He was putting Bruce's life on the line too, because if any of his pals get suspicious of him, they are going to take some revenge. And they'll be trigger-happy. They'll shoot, even if they only *think* they've seen Gregory. Or they'll spray bullets through our front windows and hit whoever is there. He hadn't thought of that." She stopped.

That was it. That was all. We went in to do our shopping, filled with our dark and sober thoughts. Later, when I left Fern at her back door, Gregory came out to help her carry in all the bags. He did not speak to me nor I to him. But as he lifted out the last bag he gave me a small tired smile. I had never seen him look so wracked. I returned his smile with a small one of my own. Then on the way home I prayed aloud. Usually I simply think my prayers. But this time I could hear my own sobbing voice. "Please, God! Help Gregory! Stay with him now! Help him to do what's right! Please, God! *Please!*"

It was the next morning and I was making my bed after breakfast when I heard a knock at my front door just as the chime sounded. I knew it was Gregory, who was always impatient. He came in quietly and stood before me as I dropped into my blue wing chair. How had he decided last night? Had he come to tell me? I had hardly slept—wondering—praying—hoping—fearing—*waiting*—

I waited now.

He spoke abruptly, his voice low and fierce. *"I can't risk Bruce! Gram! I can't!"* I could hear his hard breathing, but after a second or two he went on, a little more quietly, though his brown eyes were still blazing with a helpless anger. "I can't!" he repeated. "Don't you see I can't? I haven't any *right* to risk anybody's life but my own! But there's Bruce—*everybody!*" He stopped. Then— "And Mike. I've known Mike for eight years, Gram! How could I turn him in?" He checked himself and was suddenly quite calm and controlled. "So now I've got to get out of here. Right away."

"They're after you?"

"Will be. Something went wrong, Gram. I'll tell you. But I'd like to use your phone first."

I nodded toward it, then I left him to finish making my bed. I didn't want to hear anything. I didn't want to know anything. I couldn't think. When I joined him in a few minutes he was sitting on the sofa bed, still talking, though I had thought he was through. I heard him say, "I'll call you back as soon as I can, Jim. Maybe around three this afternoon. I can't locate Mike right now." He put down the receiver and turned to me.

"That was Jim. There was a mix-up last night. I was asking him for a chance to explain. A second chance so I could set it up again. But he'll never give it to me. Never. So I need time."

"I don't understand, Greg."

"I met them, Gram. Yes, I did. Last night. I introduced Mike to them. I'd told him all about it and we hatched up a scheme and were going to skip together. We knew they'd test the heroin Mike sold to them. But we thought it would take all today and we'd have time. But Jim called me while I was eating breakfast. He said it wasn't heroin at all. Some harmless powder. I don't understand. So I came over here to call Mike in case our phone at home is bugged. But I can't get him. He doesn't answer. I've got to tell him—ask him—" He stopped. "I don't know, Gram. I just don't know. Maybe I shouldn't have—but telling him—taking him in—was the only way I could manage. He's my *friend,* Gram!" He stopped again. "But now I don't know. It could have been a mistake on Mike's part. If he were only home so I could ask him and he could—would—explain. But I don't *know!*" He stopped once more, then a wry twisted smile touched his mouth. "I suppose if he was afraid there might be trouble, he'd rather it was *my* trouble than his." Suddenly he stood up. "I can't wait to get him. I've got a little head start now. A couple of hours anyway—" He still stood there looking at me.

I looked at him. My grandson—slender, clean, neat—and though

I saw in his eyes the bitter realization that he had come to an unexpected end of his dream, yet in some strange way he seemed undefeated. But he was waiting for me to speak.

"Where will you go, Greg?"

"I know where I'll go. Don't worry."

"You'll fly?"

"Yes."

Still he stood there waiting. I knew what he wanted and I knew he would not ask. I said, "Greg, I can't drive you to the airport. You know my old car. It keeps stalling when I shift gears and sometimes it won't go without help from a garage. If I took you, it could be disastrous for you. Call a taxi, Greg. It can get you there within an hour. Have you enough money?"

He nodded and turned to the phone again. While we waited for the cab to come I asked one more question. "What will you do when you get there?"

He whirled on me explosively. "What will I *do!* I'll get a *job!* I'll get married, and *Kay* will get a job! With *this* hanging over me, we'll go to some quiet place and live *quietly!*" Passion gathered in him. "I'll have nothing more to do with marijuana! I won't have a single joint in my possession! Not one! And I won't drive anybody's car, so I won't get any tickets and be in trouble *that* way either!" He paused. "I'll have to change my looks some, I guess."

I nodded. What he was saying, I felt sure, was that he intended to change his way of living anyway, whether he could clear his record or not. Then a horn beeped outside, Gregory swooped to kiss me, and I cried, "Call me if you get there all right, will you?" "Yes!" he answered.

"And call if you need me!" He was gone.

Love for his brother, fealty to his friend—two ennobling qualities. Yet they had been Gregory's undoing. How could God have let this happen? And what could He do now?

20

Now faith is the substance of things hoped for, the evidence of things not seen.

Hebrews 11:1

Gregory telephoned his mother instead of me, and then she called me. He had reached there all right. "Don't worry." He would get in touch with us whenever he could but he would not tell her where he was for fear her phone was bugged. He might call me instead as he thought my phone would be safe since Jim knew nothing about me. "We left it like that, Mother. He didn't say anything more." She added that Jim had called her earlier asking for Greg's whereabouts but she couldn't give him any information at that time because she knew nothing. Then Jim had said he felt badly about Gregory's disappearance, since he had believed in him. "I told him that we still did." She ended by saying that Jim had promised to call her if he got any word about him. He had had to send out orders for his arrest again. He hadn't wanted to but he had had to, because Gregory had left the state owing it five thousand dollars for his bail. "I know," Fern had answered. "He was just thinking of us." Just before Jim hung up he had asked Fern if she could tell him anything about this Mike. "Only that I have never liked or trusted him," she had answered. "Well, I'll call you," Jim said again.

However, he did not call. Nor did Gregory. And the silence grew. The days went by and still no word from either Jim or Gregory. Where was he? The days stretched into weeks and the silence continued. Had he been picked up by the police and, because he had changed his appearance, had not been recognized? If that were the case, Jim wouldn't know. About then Bruce gave Fern a disturbing rumor that had gone over the grapevine. Mike, too, was hunting for

Gregory, never having believed in Greg's plan for them both to get away together and feeling certain that Gregory had double-crossed him. He was going south soon and would find Greg and "get him."

As time dragged by I became sure that Gregory was dead. Killed by a bullet from some pursuing officer of the law. And how would we ever know? With his looks changed and no identifying papers on him —except fake ones—how indeed would we know? And we wanted the answer, whatever it was. For the strain was wearing. Still we heard nothing. We did not know Jim's last name or his address or his official position in the state, so we could not call him. We wouldn't even know him if we saw him. We could only wait. And the waiting grew more and more harrowing.

One day Fern came to see me. She said, "Mother, I've been talking to our minister. And he reminded me that we had asked God to help Gregory from the very beginning. And when he was in jail down south we had prayed to Him to change Gregory's heart. To make him over. What we have to do now is trust Him. There's nothing *we* can do, you know. I'm believing that no news is good news and that he's alive and well somewhere. So—I am giving Gregory over into God's hands. I'm asking the Lord to take care of him. Why don't you do the same thing?"

I did not reply. Presently she left me. And, sitting in my wing chair in the quiet of my living room, I began to think about what she had suggested.

Gregory had been in the hands of the Lord from the very beginning. When I had first asked him to come stay with me it had been without any volition on my part, any forethought, or indeed any real desire. My mind had told me it was a crazy thing for me to do—invite him to live with me—yet I had done it. Why? Because I couldn't help it. Because God had intended it. Because God cared enough about Gregory to make me His agent. This I had discovered the day I finally succeeded in getting Gregory admitted to the county hospital.

But later, during Gregory's second sojourn with me, God had seemed to cease caring, and Gregory's stay with me had ended in a sad fiasco. I couldn't understand why He had allowed this to happen —and because I couldn't, my faith in Him was badly shaken. As was my belief in His caring and interest and concern. And this was not restored until, half a year later, a minister, another of God's agents, had promised me that "something good" was going to happen to me, and I had believed him. Only a little while later this promise had been kept when Gregory began writing letters to us which seemed to indicate an about-face in his thinking.

Here my thoughts paused. What had happened to Gregory when we all believed he had changed? Why this heartbreaking failure now? *Why?* Three times Gregory had brought us from hope to despair. Why had we had to go through all that pain and misery if it was to reach a finish, as it had, in nothing?

Nothing. Again my thoughts paused. For the word had hit me sharply. I had said "nothing" because I had thought just that. But now I asked myself—How did I *know?* The end had not yet come. I was still waiting for it, wasn't I? So the future lay ahead. And though I couldn't see into it, surely God could. God knew what Gregory's future was to be. And Fern was telling me to trust Him. Again. And more.

A friend had once told me that my faith was founded only on emotional experience and that wasn't enough. Reason was needed. What reason had I for my belief in God's power and His constant presence?

In answer I told her about the very first night when Gregory had come to live with me and how, after welcoming him and feeding him and leaving him comfortably ensconced in his sofa bed, I had gone to my room. And how there, in an enveloping silence, I had sent up to God out of a full heart, a prayer of thanks to Him for bringing Gregory to me. For touching him in such a way that he had *wanted* to come. I had never meant a prayer more. My gratitude was so real and deep and warm that it was almost hurtful. And there in the quiet and solitude of my room I had suddenly felt sure that my words had been heard. That God, though not visible, was a presence alive with me—near me—and that He had been waiting—listening—for me to speak. Had that too been only an emotional experience? No. More than that. It was a flooding certainty. A *knowing.* Reason had no part in it. Reason had not been around. Reason had not been needed. Because what I had felt was stronger than reason. It was—simply—truth.

And this truth, as I have come to know it, was something that, in spite of its unsteady course, I grew to feel I must tell the world. At first, when I had been urged to write of my experience with Gregory, I had refused. I had lived it. That was enough. I had no desire to go through all that agony again, as I would have to should I write of it. But the idea would not let me alone. It nagged at me. So, finally, I wrote it. I wrote it three times, never satisfied, never knowing just why I persisted. Why, I asked myself, need I feel I must tell the tale of all that work and worry which, after all, had had no happy ending? As I sat there in my living room, an answer came—as so many had—quietly. And I saw with a slow dawning astonishment that while I had thought I would bring Gregory into a right way of living and so to God, it was really through Gregory that God brought me home to Him. Perhaps the whole point and purpose of my long unusual relationship with him was just that. Was it not, after all, then, in a sense and in a totally unexpected way, a "good ending"? And given to me, in spite of himself, by Gregory. Yes, I was the good ending. Even so, God would go on working in Gregory's life in other ways through other people until he too might realize his need for the Lord. My Lord.

Darling Gregory! I loved him so! Now more than ever. In one way he was a little like me. I had been full of confidence and sure I could establish the pattern of our days together. But I hadn't been able to work it out and, in desperation, I had turned to God for help. First, in humility, I had acknowledged my incompetence, and *then* I had asked. And it had been given—but not when or how I had expected it, rather in a way and at an hour of God's own choosing.

All this was something Gregory had not yet learned. In his struggle against methadone long ago, he had battled alone, sure of his strength. But it hadn't been enough. And just recently in his struggle against the forces of evil which he knew so well, he had again battled alone, still sure of his strength. As before, however, it wasn't enough. If he had just asked for help from God! But he hadn't. I had. Fern had. But never Gregory. He did not understand that God set conditions. He did not yet know he must ask first. "Behold, I stand at the door and knock: if any man hear my voice, and open the door, I will come in to him . . ." (Revelation 3:20).

Yes, Gregory must hear His voice and answer. He must ask. And until he is ready within himself to ask— Ah! That was it. He wasn't ready. And God knew it.

It was then that I clasped my hands together in my lap, put my head back, closed my eyes, and spoke aloud:

"Dear God! Hear me, please. First I want to thank You for this experience I have had with Gregory, because it has brought me to You. Because, through him, I have learned so much about You. I have learned to believe. And to trust. I have seen the workings of Your ways that prove Your continual interest and caring. I ask You now to be with Gregory in the time ahead. Help him to find the right path. Help him discover what he needs to know and do in order to get Your help. Guide him as You have guided me and help him sense Your guidance. Bless those who, instead of me, will be Your agents in his behalf. Take care of him, I beg of you. And give him a good ending, too, in the book of his life. I cannot see or imagine what that ending will be. But You can. You know. And You can work miracles as You have before. You can change hearts. You can transform thoughts. You can lead to new ways. I ask You now to do this for Gregory in Your own way and at Your own time when he is ready. And so I am giving him into Your hands, dear Lord, knowing You will help him as he needs to be helped. I give him into Your keeping gladly. In hope. In trust. Amen."

I opened my eyes and picked up my Bible, which is always on a small stand next to my chair. At random I opened it and found this verse: "Therefore being justified by faith, we have peace with God through our Lord Jesus Christ" (Romans 5:1).

Peace. Yes. I have peace in my heart at last.

Thank You, God.